Star Trek and Star Wars

PETER LANG
PROMPT

PETER LANG
New York • Berlin • Brussels • Lausanne • Oxford

George A. Gonzalez

Star Trek and Star Wars

The Enlightenment versus the Anti-Enlightenment

PETER LANG
New York • Berlin • Brussels • Lausanne • Oxford

Library of Congress Cataloging-in-Publication Control Number: 2022026941

Bibliographic information published by **Die Deutsche Nationalbibliothek.**
Die Deutsche Nationalbibliothek lists this publication in the "Deutsche
Nationalbibliografie"; detailed bibliographic data are available
on the Internet at http://dnb.d-nb.de/.

ISBN 978-1-4331-9770-3 (hardcover)
ISBN 978-1-4331-9771-0 (ebook pdf)
ISBN 978-1-4331-9772-7 (epub)
DOI 10.3726/b19760

This publication has been peer reviewed and meets
the highest quality standards for content and production.

© 2022 Peter Lang Publishing, Inc., New York
29 Broadway, 18th floor, New York, NY 10006
www.peterlang.com

For Jonathan P. West (who will forever be missed)

Contents

Introduction

The Enlightenment is predicated on two fundamental assumptions. First, there is a big picture (or meta-narrative) to any political system – politics/(in)justice (at the highest levels) is knowable. We can attain truth/knowledge of the political world through reason and empiricism. Second, the broader public is capable of collectively shaping the big picture (meta-narrative) of society – and should do so (democracy). The presumption is that people (again, collectively) desire justice/fairness for all (universalism), as well as the public good.[1] Indeed, it is the public's demands over the course of history that has moved the world toward regimes based on legal equality – a rejection of aristocracy/monarchy/colonialism.

There is what can be labeled as an anti-Enlightenment outlook. The most significant aspect of the anti-Enlightenment is there is no meta-narrative to the operation of society. Politics is only about the maintenance of stability (social order). Societal progress (to the extent that it

---

1 Jedediah Britton-Purdy, "We're Not a Real Democracy. That's Why Jan. 6 Happened," *New York Times*, Jan. 6, 2022, A23.

occurs) is solely a function of technology and not a perfecting of justice/ fairness. Because people lack sufficient knowledge of the world, democracy may not be the appropriate means of making political decisions.

As I note below, popular culture (television, movies) is the democratization of art. With popular culture, the Enlightenment and anti-Enlightenment are put before the broad public. Hence, popular culture is praxis – the application, practice of political philosophy (i.e., the Enlightenment versus the anti-Enlightenment). Star Trek is arguably the popular culture vehicle most reflective of the Enlightenment (Chapter One). The Star Wars franchise is seemingly the artistic embodiment of the anti-Enlightenment (Chapter Two). The Star Trek series of the 1960s was not simply metaphorical of the Enlightenment, but directly participated (even led) in the civil rights and feminist movements of the era (Chapter Three). With former President Donald J. Trump (2017–2021) openly courting the forces of hate,[2] it is appropriate to revisit the 1950s (Trump's slogan of "Make America Great Again" a.k.a. MAGA) – when hate (of communism – *anti-communism*) was politically dominant in the U.S. (Chapter Four). The anti-communist regime of hate in America resulted in the U.S. war in Vietnam (1965–1973) – whereby the American military measured success by the number of enemy ("communists") dead.[3] Star Trek (as Enlightenment popular culture) warns against the anti-Enlightenment – Samuel Huntington's *Clash of Civilizations* ideation (Chapter Five). In Chapter Six I argue that *Man in the High Castle* (a series about a Nazi conquest of America) reflects the pessimism/demoralization underlying the Trump phenomenon – the rise of (anti-democratic) virulent nationalism.

2 Michael D. Shear, "Trump Amplifies 'White Power' on Twitter," *New York Times*, June 29, 2020, A15; Nicholas Kristof, "Trump Calls On Extremists To 'Stand By'," *New York Times*, Oct. 1, 2020, A27; Alan Feuer, "Testimony of Trump Allies And Extremists at Hearing," *New York Times*, June 30, 2022, A17.
3 Harry G. Summers, "Body Count Proved to Be a False Prophet," *Los Angeles Times*, Feb. 9, 1991, A5; Gregory A. Daddis, *Westmoreland's War: Reassessing American Strategy in Vietnam* (New York: Oxford University Press, 2014).

Chapter One

The Hegel/Marx Political Philosophy Paradigm

The political philosophy of the Hegel/Marx paradigm is composed of a four-part methodology: (1) Mediation, (2) Totality, (3) Genesis, and (4) Praxis.[1] These components inform our understanding of what Georg Hegel (1770–1831) labels the "Whole" – otherwise referred to the as the *Absolute*.[2] All four components of this methodology will be treated herein – with Praxis being specifically addressed in Chapter Two. I will start with two broad points: the methodology operates dialectically (as is to be fully expected with Hegelian/Marxist reasoning). Thus, mediation -> totality -> genesis -> praxis – the process also operates in reverse and interactively overall. Again, this is textbook Hegel/Marx. A second

---

1 Georg Lukács, *History and Class Consciousness*, trans. Rodney Livingstone (Cambridge, MA: MIT Press, 1971 [1922]); Daniel Andrés López, *Lukács: Praxis and the Absolute* (Chicago: Haymarket Books, 2020).
2 Donald Phillip Verene, *Hegel's Absolute: An Introduction to Reading the Phenomenology of Spirit* (Albany: State University New York Press, 2007); James Kreines, *Reason in the World: Hegel's Metaphysics and its Philosophical Appeal* (New York: Oxford University Press, 2015); George A. Gonzalez, *The Absolute and Star Trek* (New York: Palgrave Macmillan, 2017).

point I want to emphasize is that in the realm of praxis art is salient.[3] Praxis is the application, practice of Hegel/Marxist theorizing, speculation. Praxis, however, is more than the application of such theorizing, speculation. Praxis communicates knowledge of the "whole". Put differently, praxis in a sense stands alone in the dialectic – as it confirms or disproves the other aspects of the dialectic and, as a result, it is a source of knowledge.

Hegel himself held that philosophy, religion, and art were sources of knowledge of the Whole. During Hegel's time he came to conclude that art was no longer a source of knowledge as it had become ossified and an instrument of the religious, political hierarchy.[4] Art, however, has been revitalized as it has been de-linked from religious, political institutions. This de-linking has taken the form of popular culture.

Hegel and Karl Marx (1818–1883) clearly stood in the Enlightenment tradition[5] – perhaps they most clearly represent it (the inexorable progress/*elevation*/enlightening of society/humanity). There are also philosophers that stand opposed to the Enlightenment – so-called anti-Enlightenment thinkers.[6] Praxis through popular culture occurs both in terms of expressing the Enlightenment and the anti-Enlightenment. The Star Trek franchise (in all of popular culture) most lucidly depicts the Enlightenment and its practice (the Idea – discussed below). The popularity of Star Trek indicates that it is knowledge of the Whole.[7]

---

3 George A. Gonzalez, *Popular Culture as Art and Knowledge* (Lanham, MD: Lexington Books, 2019); Robert B. Pippin, *Philosophy by Other Means: The Arts in Philosophy and Philosophy in the Arts* (Chicago: University of Chicago Press, 2021).
4 Jack Kaminsky, *Hegel on Art: An Interpretation of Hegel's Aesthetics* (Albany: State University of New York Press, 1970).
5 Jonathan I. Israel, *Radical Enlightenment: Philosophy and the Making of Modernity, 1650–1750* (New York: Oxford University Press, 2001), and *Enlightenment Contested: Philosophy, Modernity, and the Emancipation of Man, 1670–1752* (New York: Oxford University Press, 2006).
6 Ronald Beiner, *Dangerous Minds: Nietzsche, Heidegger, and the Return of the Far Right* (Philadelphia: University of Pennsylvania Press, 2018); Richard Wolin, *The Seduction of Unreason: The Intellectual Romance with Fascism from Nietzsche to Postmodernism*, 2nd ed. (Princeton: Princeton University Press, 2019); John S. Huntington, *Far-Right Vanguard: The Radical Roots of Modern Conservatism* (Philadelphia: University of Pennsylvania Press, 2021).
7 Gonzalez, *The Absolute and Star Trek*.

Popular Culture as Knowledge

During the Renaissance (in conjunction with the rise of the Enlightenment), art (paintings, sculptures) failed in the 14th to early 19th centuries to adequately, and fully reflect the humanism and rationality that was becoming dominant – as manifest by the American (1775–1783) and French Revolutions (1789). Instead, art (particularly in the artistically dominant European scene) was entrenched within religious, mythological motifs.[8] This is not to deny that art during this period became more sophisticated and beautiful (one wants to say impassioned) in presenting arguments supportive of religion (Christianity) and the aristocracy. Nevertheless, art in this context can be viewed as a rearguard action by hegemonic elites to counter the enlightenment process that was taking place. The art world in this period was dominated by wealthy patrons and wealthy connoisseurs – not to mention the official and brutal censorship at the time.[9]

With movies and television, art (culture) took a decidedly popular turn. For popular culture to reach/affect the public, it has to be authentic. Put differently, to get people to watch movies and television shows, they have to appeal to them (i.e., they have to be popular). Popular culture can be deemed the democratization of culture – art for the masses. Thus, even though the movie and television industries are dominated by major, behemoth corporations and the Billionaires that own and control them,[10] popular culture cannot solely reflect their outlook, political/social preferences. Instead, popular culture (to a significant degree) must convey broader reasoning on political/social phenomena, and even be a venue of critique of hegemonic groups, institutions.

---

8 Evelyn Welch, *Art in Renaissance Italy: 1350–1500* (New York: Oxford University Press, 2001); Susie Nash, *Northern Renaissance Art* (New York: Oxford University Press, 2009).

9 James Simpson, *Permanent Revolution: The Reformation and the Illiberal Roots of Liberalism* (Cambridge, MA: Belknap Press, 2019); Eric Berkowitz, *Dangerous Ideas: A Brief History of Censorship in the West, from the Ancients to Fake News* (Boston: Beacon Press, 2021).

10 Eli M. Noam, and The International Media Concentration Collaboration, *Who Owns the World's Media?: Media Concentration and Ownership around the World* (New York: Oxford University Press, 2016).

A recent salient example of such critique is the animated movie *Superman: Red Son* (2020). In this iteration of the Superman franchise the "Man of Steel" is a Soviet citizen and an adherent of the October Revolution. Superman comes to learn of Stalin's perfidy and murders him – taking over leadership of the country. Superman ends Stalinist repression, but the regime uses mind control to maintain obedience and in the end the "Soviet empire" is dissolved. The distinctive critique in the movie is that of American foreign policy. Under the leadership of capitalist Lex Luther, the U.S. carries out unprovoked aggression against the Soviet Union (a.k.a. the USSR) – a false flag downing of a satellite on Manhattan and unleashing "superheroes" against it (thereby attacking the USSR). Perhaps especially significant, Luther develops a "Superior Man" to counter Superman. When Superior Man is introduced to the public he declares "America First" – suggesting that U.S. anti-Soviet policy (anti-communism) at the center of the Cold War was informed by virulent nationalism (see Chapter Four).[11] The German Nazis would similarly like to emphasize "Germany above all else" (Deutschland über alles).[12] In actual history the U.S. did attack the Soviet Union in the context of the country's civil war,[13] violated its air space with spy planes,[14] and maintained a hostile foreign policy toward the USSR in the form of an aggressive military posture.[15] In *Red Son* the Berlin Wall is deployed by the West – a metaphor for the anti-Soviet policy of *containment*?[16] (see Chapter Four).

During the actual Cold War (circa. 1950 to circa. 1989), *Star Trek* (1966–1969), in the episode "Private Little War" (1968), the argument is made that the American involvement in Vietnam was not about justice

11 George A. Gonzalez, *Star Trek and Popular Culture: Television at the Frontier of Social and Political Change in the 1960s* (New York: Peter Lang, 2021), chap. 2.
12 Daniel A. Gross, "'Deutschland über Alles' and 'America First,' in Song," *New Yorker*, February 18, 2017. Web.
13 James Carl Nelson, *The Polar Bear Expedition: The Heroes of America's Forgotten Invasion of Russia, 1918–1919* (New York: William Morrow, 2019).
14 Monte Reel, *A Brotherhood of Spies: The U-2 and the CIA's Secret War* (New York: Doubleday, 2018).
15 Robert J. McMahon, *The Cold War: A Very Short Introduction*, 2nd ed. (New York: Oxford University Press, 2021).
16 John Lewis Gaddis, *Strategies of Containment: A Critical Appraisal of Postwar American National Security Policy* (New York: Oxford University Press, 1982).

but about maintaining stability between the great powers of the era ("Balance of Power"). Captain Kirk renders substantive (detached) commentary on the Vietnam War in "Private Little War": "do you remember the 20th century brush wars on the Asian continent?" In discussing the war Kirk finds fault with both the U.S. and the USSR in using Vietnam as a battlefield in their great power competition: "Two giant powers involved ... Neither side could pull out." Kirk holds that the U.S. (along with the USSR) is involved in the "dirtiest game of them all" in Vietnam – "Balance of Power". Another original series episode, a Kligon commander observes (ostensibly referencing the great power politics of the time): "You of the Federation, you are much like us [the Kligons]. . . . Two tigers, predators, hunters, killers."[17] While Kirk notes that the American war effort in Vietnam is not about justice (but stability), it is still the case that in seeking "balance" in Vietnam the U.S. engaged in wholly brutal policies. In the context of where the American military command measured success in Vietnam by the number of enemy dead,[18] Doctor McCoy's observation in "Private Little War" that "killing is stupid and useless" is a powerful, unequivocal condemnation.

For art, popular culture to play the role of generating knowledge of the Whole artistic freedom is central.[19] Therefore, the recent and ongoing threat to democratic norms in the U.S. (in particular)[20] is a profound threat to the ability of the artist (creators of movies and television shows) to explore, and convey the Whole – its four aspects: Mediation, Totality, Genesis, Praxis.

It is important to note that while authoritarian regimes can block the exploration, depiction of the Whole, there is no evidence that popular culture can successfully be used to induce hate, and backwardness.

---

17 (*Star Trek*, original series – "Errand of Mercy" 1967).

18 Harry G. Summers, "Body Count Proved to Be a False Prophet," *Los Angeles Times*, Feb. 9, 1991, A5.

19 Jacob Mchangama, *Free Speech: A History from Socrates to Social Media* (New York: Basic Books, 2022).

20 Jamelle Bouie, "The Trump Conspiracy Is Hiding in Plain Sight," *New York Times*, Dec. 5, 2021, SR7; Maggie Haberman, Alexandra Berzon, and Michael S. Schmidt, "Trump's Allies Keep Up Fight To Nullify Vote," *New York Times*, April 19, 2022, A1; Adam Liptak, and Nick Corasaniti, "Supreme Court Could Reshape Election Rules," *New York Times*, July 1, 2022, A1.

Put differently and more precisely, popular culture cannot be used in an instrumental manner. Elsewhere I present an analysis of cinema produced under the authority of the German Nazi regime (1933–1945). What is demonstrated is that while the Nazi leadership was strongly intent on using popular culture to indoctrinate the public with their hateful, myopic outlook, and values (the Jewish Cabal, the Leader Cult, the Aryan Race), they were unable to present their politics through the movies.[21]

Mediation

Mediation for Hegel and Marx begins with the notion that human civilization is a totality. Hegel drew this conclusion through his experience of the French Revolution. Virtually overnight (with the resulting Napoleonic wars of the late 18th century) politics on the European continent shifted from feudal conceptions of personal fealty to the Kaiser, etc., to conceptions of popular sovereignty, citizenship, the rights of individuals, fair procedures, etc. This decisive shift away from a personalized social order toward a liberal (legalistic) one began with the American Revolution – "All Men are Created Equal". With this Hegel reasoned that political ideas, norms collectively shifted (the totality). Such shifts are proof positive of the Whole or the Absolute (where normative values inhere). Hegel further pointed to the fact that major (collective) shifts in human political values (revolutions) had occurred in the past (genesis)[22] – leading to the endpoint of constitutional monarchy (praxis). Hegel has been criticized for holding that the endpoint of his telos was a constitutional monarchy (hardly a fully rational, liberating outcome). In fairness to Hegel when he was writing his home country of Prussia was under the absolutist control of the Kaiser and to even suggest that rational government was constitutional monarchy was personally and professionally perilous – Hegel was a philosophy professor. Even if we can fault Hegel for his limited version of political

21 Gonzalez, *Popular Culture as Art and Knowledge*, chap. 2.
22 Daniel Lee, *The Right of Sovereignty: Jean Bodin on the Sovereign State and the Law of Nations* (New York: Oxford University Press, 2021).

equality, it is still the case that Hegel argued that a fairer, more just (rights based) future would come to fruition.[23]

Marx took Hegel's concept of praxis further and argued that a rational society is one that is modern, classless, and totally free of ethnic and gender biases.[24] An endpoint of the Whole is this Idea, or the contemporary conception of justice. Perhaps more significantly, to Hegel's Idealism (the notion that society's political shifts are primarily the product of the evolution of ideas) Marx added a decisively materialist component. Specifically, Marx held that societal politics are directly reflective of its productive capacities. What can be read into Marx's formulation is that as humanity's productive capacity advances, the more free and equal society becomes – with modern industrialization (mass production) allowing for true equality (whereby everyone can fully, meaningfully engage culture, art, philosophy, etc.).

A significant twist in Marx's reasoning (to put it somewhat mildly) is that capitalism (in particular) is an economic/political system rife with instability and crisis. Thus, whereby earlier societal epochs (slavery, feudal) lasted millennia – capitalism will be comparatively short-lived. Marx foresaw the race to the bottom initiated by the increasing, ongoing automation of production. The greater and greater costs of building technologically advanced industry meant finance capital would over time demand cheaper and cheaper production factors, platforms to maximize investment returns (thereby distributing wealth upwards).[25] This made capitalism inherently economically and politically unstable – cycling through one political and economic crisis after another, as wealth became more and more concentrated.[26] Contemporary politics, events makes Marx's political economy arguments with regard to capitalism especially compelling. With global neoliberalism (the free

---

23 Peter Singer, *Hegel: A Very Short Introduction* (New York: Oxford University Press, 2001).
24 Tom Rockmore, *Marx's Dream: From Capitalism to Communism* (Chicago: University of Chicago Press, 2018).
25 Ruth Whippman,"We're All in Sales Now," *New York Times*, Nov. 25, 2018, SR1; David Leonhardt, "When C.E.O.s Cared About America," *New York Times*, Dec. 3, 2018, A27.
26 Peter Singer, *Marx: A Very Short Introduction* (New York: Oxford University Press, 2001).

international of movement of capital, goods, and services),[27] wealth has become especially concentrated (the Billionaire Class)[28] and crises afflict the entirety of the world's economy (e.g., the Great Recession of 2008).[29]

Marx's conception of revolution, however, needs to be de-linked from his theorizing of the perpetual crises of capitalism. Beyond capitalism, Marx wrote about *communism*. As I have noted elsewhere, Marx may have been too sanguine about the crises ("contradictions") of capitalism resulting in a society of ideal justice – a modern classless society, totally free of ethnic, gender biases (i.e., communism).[30] Hence, it is left for Rosa Luxemburg (1871–1919) to opine that the future is either "socialism or barbarism".[31] I outline in *The Absolute and Star Trek* that the franchise posits that people must possess the correct attitudes in order to bring about an ideal socialist society: (1) a commitment to social justice; (2) an unyielding commitment to the truth; and (3) a similar commitment to scientific, intellectual discovery.[32] The embracing of these outlooks (frames of thought) is the only way that people can "see" the *absolute* and bring it fully to fruition.

A fictional collective shift in public reasoning toward social justice is outlined in the *Star Trek* (original series) episode "City on the Edge of Forever" (1967). Captain Kirk explains to Edith Keeler in the context of the 1930s that *"Let me help. A hundred years or so from now a famous novelist will write a classic using that theme. He'll recommend those three words even over I love you."* The diminishment of *I love you* reflects the rejection of the kind of self-centeredness emblematic of capitalism – in other words, the individual's desire for love (to love and be

27 David Harvey, *A Brief History of Neoliberalism* (New York: Oxford University Press, 2007); Gary Gerstle, *The Rise and Fall of the Neoliberal Order: America and the World in the Free Market Era* (New York: Oxford University Press, 2022).

28 Benjamin I. Page, Jason Seawright, and Matthew J. Lacombe, *Billionaires and Stealth Politics* (Chicago: University of Chicago Press, 2018); Peter S. Goodman, *Davos Man: How the Billionaires Devoured the World* (New York: Custom House, 2022).

29 David Harvey, *Seventeen Contradictions and the End of Capitalism* (New York: Oxford University Press, 2014), and *Marx, Capital, and the Madness of Economic Reason* (New York: Oxford University Press, 2017).

30 Harvey, *Seventeen Contradictions and the End of Capitalism*.

31 Stephen Eric Bronner, *Rosa Luxemburg: A Revolutionary for Our Times* (University Park: Pennsylvania State University Press, 1993).

32 Gonzalez, *The Absolute and Star Trek*, 2–3.

loved), wealth, prestige, personal power. This kind of self-regarding is at the core of instrumental reason.[33] The embrace of *let me help* over *I love you* is to center human consciousness on societal well-being – spurning individual aggrandizement (ego-gratification) in favor of the welfare of others, society.

Luxemburg made her proclamation about the future ("socialism or barbarism") in the early 20th century (1915) – during World War One. Standing in the early 21st two lessons can be drawn from the 20th century – firstly, it is evident that progressive (communist) revolution and the crises of capitalism are indeed de-linked; secondly, we have a clearer understanding of the *barbarism* that Luxemburg forewarned. One possible barbarism we now fully comprehend is global warming. In this way, human understanding of technology and engineering is outpacing our norms, policies of establishing a sustainable relationship with nature. Redolent of this reality is a point made by Captain Kirk in the fictional 23rd century (ostensibly referencing the Cold War of the 1960s – e.g., the Cuban Missile Crisis): "There came a time when our weapons grew faster than our wisdom, and we almost destroyed ourselves" ("Private Little War").

The other prime lesson of the 20th century is that capitalist crisis (the kind envisioned by Marx) can result in Nazism/fascism. The failure of German capitalism in the early 20th century led to a Nazi regime that unleashed horrific war and genocide. Thus, the German working class ended up enacting a violently destructive war and a deranged agenda (the Holocaust) as part of the effort to overcome the economic depression/devastation of the 1920s and 1930s. Any country today falling to a (delusional) Nazi regime can (almost certainly will) initiate a nuclear conflagration. *Star Trek* "City on the Edge of Forever" posits the idea that a Nazi victory in World War Two would have meant the end of civilization.

Hence, again, we must analytically bifurcate progressive revolution from the inherent instability of contemporary capitalism.

---

33 Darrow Schecter, *The Critique of Instrumental Reason from Weber to Habermas* (New York: Bloomsbury Academic, 2012); Max Horkheimer, *Critique of Instrumental Reason*, trans. Matthew O'Connell (New York: Verso, 2013 [1974]).

Understanding that capitalist crisis is seemingly just as likely to result in societal collapse (barbarism) as it is in communism (total justice[34]), the question facing humanity in the present epoch is how to avoid the former and achieve the latter? There is more than ample evidence (discussed below) to conclude that the Whole is inexorably drawing humanity to the Idea of total justice as envisioned by Marx. The problem that humanity faces is that powerful forces are actively trying to stop the "elevation" of humanity (i.e., its advancing intellectual, emotional maturity, sophistication).[35] The specific issue is can humans (the *totality*) achieve sufficient (social, political) elevation (in the face of elite machinations, skullduggery[36]) before it is too late and civilization collapses into barbarism (or humanity is altogether eliminated)?[37]

Totality

With regard to the social/political evolution (or ongoing *elevation*) of humanity, this is outlined in the Star Trek franchise. Interestingly, in the Star Trek franchise the evolving rationality, maturity of humanity is referred to most explicitly in *Star Trek: The Animated Series* (1973-1974). The episode "The Magicks of Megas-Tu" (1973) invokes the Salem witch trials. Old world "devils, warlocks, evil sorcerers" were the misunderstood, maligned, massacred aliens (Megans) that the Enterprise was now encountering. The Megans, now fearful of humans, place Kirk *et al.* on trial: "These are the defendants, as representatives of the vilest species in all the universe, treacherous humanity." In humanity's defense Kirk explains: "in the centuries since the Salem witch trials we have

---

34 Todd McGowan, *Universality and Identity Politics* (New York: Columbia University Press, 2020).

35 Berkowitz, *Dangerous Ideas.*

36 George A. Gonzalez, "Is Obama's 2014 Greenhouse Gas Reduction Plan Symbolic?: The Creation of the U.S. EPA and a Reliance on the States," *Capitalism Nature Socialism* 26 (2015) no. 2: 92–104, and *Energy, the Modern State, and the American World System* (Albany: State University of New York Press, 2018); Lisa Friedman, and Jonathan Weisman, "G.O.P. Strategy for Climate Action Is to Delay It," *New York Times*, July 21, 2022, A1.

37 Livia Albeck-Ripka, "A 'Black Box' for an Earth At Risk of a Climate Crash," *New York Times*, Dec. 11, 2021, A8; David E. Sanger, "Scientists Urge President To Slash Nuclear Arsenal," *New York Times*, Dec. 17, 2021, A16.

learned. We try to understand and respect all life forms. . . . The records of the Enterprise are open for your inspection. All the history of Earth and the Federation is at your disposal." In an effort to tap into the prejudices of humans, the Enterprise crew is told that the one Megan that has befriended, protected them is no less than "the Rollicker, the Tempter, Lucifer" himself. Kirk, reflecting modern, secular, humane reasoning, retorts: "We're not interested in legend. He's a living being, and an intelligent life form. That's all we have to know about him. We will not join in harming him." The Megans decide to imprison Lucifer for eternity for aiding the Enterprise. Kirk risks death to protect, and help Lucifer: "I have to, or you'll become as bad as the Earthmen you fear. You're acting out of terror instead of out of thought or respect." This convinces the aliens that humans have indeed evolved: "The Megans had to have proof that mankind had grown and learned wisdom since they last saw Earth. Your compassion was that proof, Captain." "The Eye of the Beholder" (1974) is an episode where Kirk *et al.* end up as specimens in the zoo of a highly advanced species. Ultimately, Kirk's captors conclude that the Enterprise crew doesn't belong in a zoo because humans "are considered simplistic, but in the process of evolving into a higher order." Spock (who can engage in telepathic communication with the aliens) goes on to explain "it seems they were where we are some tens of thousands of centuries ago." Similarly, in the episode "Bem" (1974) an advanced alien creature recognizes that humans have evolved in terms of rationality, intellect: (to Kirk *et al.*):

> Punishment? What is punishment? Revenge? Intelligent beings need no revenge. Punishment is necessary only where learning cannot occur without it. You are behind that. My children here [a primitive peoples the entity oversees] are not. That is why you must leave, so as not to corrupt their development with concepts that they are not yet ready for.

The dichotomy between ancient people and modern humanity is again referenced in "How Sharper Than A Serpent's Tooth" (1974). A powerful creature (Kukulkan) that visited Earth thousands of years ago is again visiting Earth and demanding the deference (worship) that he received from primitive humans: "You are my children. I hoped I could teach you, help you." Kirk: "You did, long ago, when it was needed most. Our people were children then. Kukulkan, we've grown up now. We don't need you anymore." Realizing the validity of Kirk's argument, Kukulkan, deflated: "I will let you go your own way. I have already done what I can."

The Star Trek franchise also depicts political, military elites seeking to suppress the elevation of humanity. Episode "Transfigurations" (1990 – *Next Generation*): "John Doe", as he regains his memories and bearings, is finally able to transform into seemingly the *whole* – the absolute. (John: "my species is on the verge of a wondrous evolutionary change. A transmutation beyond our physical being. I am the first of my kind to approach this metamorphosis." "My people are about to embark upon a new realm, a new plane of existence.") The character is cast as possessing a quality of peace and kindness. (Dr. Crusher to John: "I don't believe you're capable of harming any[one].")

In contrast to John Doe, who seemingly achieves the ideal balance between emotion and reason (or zen) and ostensibly comes to completely know (perhaps become) the absolute, Commander Sunad of Zalkon – who demands John be killed – is dominated by "fear" of social change. ("The Zalkonians are afraid of John.") They are fearful that John's transformation is subversive. Sunad charges that John "is a disruptive influence. He spreads lies. He encourages dissent. He disturbs the natural order of our society." (John: Zalkon's "leaders . . . claimed we were dangerous so they destroyed anyone who exhibited the signs of the transfiguration.")

Sunad's fear prevents him from embracing the fact that John has achieved a higher plane of existence, and when John offers him the knowledge of this existence ("Let me show you") Sunad rejects it ("Don't touch me!"). Sunad "feels personally threatened by John." Thus, Sunad's instrumental reason[38] (i.e., his desire for political authority; high social status; and social/political stability as an end unto itself) prevents him from literally seeing/knowing the absolute.

The original series episode "Cloud Minders" (1969) depicts a society (the planet of Ardana) where torture technology ("the rays") and racism

---

38 Schecter, *The Critique of Instrumental Reason*; Horkheimer, *Critique of Instrumental Reason*.

are used to suppress opposition to a caste system. In effective imagery the political/economic/social realities of the planet are portrayed – with the privileged/governing caste living a life of aesthetic splendor in a "cloud city" ("Stratos") floating in the heavens; on the (barren) planet surface are where the laboring classes (referred to as "Troglytes") live – working the mines (extracting "zenite"). The residents of Stratos are fair-skinned and fair-haired and partake in the high arts. The Troglytes are dark-haired, dark-skinned, and unwashed.

"The rays" are deployed in an effort to break a political movement seeking to change/reform the governing regime. A Troglyte prisoner is pressed to provide the names of the putative leaders of the worker/mining caste's rebellion: "You still refuse to disclose the names of the other Disrupters." "There are no Disrupters!" "Very well, if you prefer the rays." She screams in agony, discomforting onlookers. Spock, in his famous calm, equanimous voice, observes that "Violence in reality is quite different from theory."

> But what else can [Troglytes] understand, Mister Spock?
> All the little things you and I understand and expect from life, such as equality, kindness, justice.
> Troglytes are not like Stratos dwellers, Mister Spock. They're a conglomerate of inferior species.

When the government of Adrana is told of technology that could allow for the full equality of Troglytes, it rejects this technology arguing that such a proposal "could only cause more unrest among" the Troglytes. Adrana's leader complains that (because of Kirk's efforts at reform) he "knows nothing except how to destroy our power."

Glaringly, Donald J. Trump, as U.S. President (2017–2021), declaimed *"that America will never be a socialist country"*[39] – thereby manifesting a hate of social justice. Additionally, as President, Trump openly promoted (twittered) "white power"[40] – i.e., racism. Trump actively animated far right elements throughout his presidency – culminating

---

39 As quoted in Anita Kumar "Decoding Trump's speech before the United Nations," *Politico*, Sept. 24, 2019. Web.
40 Michael D. Shear, "Trump Amplifies 'White Power' on Twitter," *New York Times*, June 29, 2020, A15.

with the storming of the U.S. Capitol Building on Jan. 6th, 2021.[41] More broadly, Republican elected leaders have recently threatened with violence those they perceive as advocates for "socialism" – again, social justice.[42] The third season (2021) of the Amazon Prime series *Hanna* (2019 to present) depicts a secret government program targeting 20 twenty-something year olds for assassination because they are perceived as potential ("subversive"[43]) leaders of future change – the presumed theory is to preemptively kill would-be V.I. Lenins, Leon Trotskys, etc.

Genesis

The *genesis* (origins) of elite efforts to stop/suppress social progress (justice) of course has an ancient history. Marx, in the *Communist Manifesto*, holds the very beginning of hegemonic (conservative) classes occurred with the advent of intellectual labor – versus physical labor. In the contemporary period capitalist elites can be perceived as suffering from myopia created by *wealth addiction*.[44] Sam Polk, a former Wall Street trader, in 2014 published an op-ed piece in the *New York Times* where he argues "wealth addiction" is rampant among the upper echelon of the American financial community.[45] Prior to coming to Wall Street Polk was a recovering drug addict. This experience as a drug addict, he

41 Adam Goldman, and Shaila Dewan, "Shouting, Smashed Glass, A Lunge, Then a Gunshot," *New York Times*, Jan. 24, 2021, A1; Peter Baker, "Increasingly Unhinged as Power Slipped Away," *New York Times*, June 29, 2022, A1; Alan Feuer, "A Few Main Characters Form the Core of the Committee's Narrative," *New York Times*, June 10, 2022, A16, and "Proud Boys Ignored Orders Given at Pre-Jan. 6 Meeting," *New York Times*, June 27, 2022, A24; Luke Broadwater, and Michael S. Schmidt, "Insider's Account of a President's Volatility," *New York Times*, June 29, 2022, A1.
42 Editorial Board, "Ms. Greene Is Beyond the Pale," *New York Times*, Feb. 1, 2021, A20; Jonathan Weisman, and Catie Edmondson, "Republican Censured By a Divided House For a Violent Video," *New York Times*, Nov. 18, 2021, A14; Jonathan Weisman, "Boebert's Call to Ilhan Over 'Suicide Bomber' Remark Shows Chasm Between Parties," *New York Times*, Nov. 30, 2021, A20; Alan Feuer, "Gun-Toting Candidate's Ad Suggests Hunt for 'RINOs'," *New York Times*, June 21, 2022, A17.
43 (*Hanna* – "Look Me In the Eye" 2021).
44 Philip E. Slater, *Wealth Addiction* (New York: Dutton, 1980). Also see George A. Gonzalez, *Popular Culture and the Political Values of Neoliberalism* (Lanham, MD: Lexington Books, 2019).
45 Sam Polk, "For the Love of Money," *New York Times*, Jan. 19, 2014, SR1.

argues, allowed him to see and diagnosis himself and others as literally addicted to wealth. Polk describes that even as he was making millions he "was a giant fireball of greed." "I wanted a billion dollars. It's staggering to think that in the course of five years, I'd gone from being thrilled at my first bonus — $40,000 — to being disappointed when, my second year at the hedge fund, I was paid 'only' $1.5 million." Polk explains that "in the end, it was actually my absurdly wealthy bosses who helped me see the limitations of unlimited wealth." Polk was taken aback by their hostility to any effort to limit their amassing of wealth – even if such efforts could strengthen the financial system. (Polk quotes one of his unnamed superiors as stating: "I don't have the brain capacity to think about the system as a whole. All I'm concerned with is how this affects our company.") Polk concludes that his boss "was afraid of losing money, despite all that he had" and begins to determine that such fears were rooted in addiction:

> From that moment on, I started to see Wall Street with new eyes. I noticed the vitriol that traders directed at the government for limiting bonuses after the crash [of 2008]. I heard the fury in their voices at the mention of higher taxes. These traders despised anything or anyone that threatened their bonuses. Ever see what a drug addict is like when he's used up his junk? He'll do anything — walk 20 miles in the snow, rob a grandma — to get a fix. Wall Street was like that.

Polk holds that upon leaving Wall Street he suffered "withdrawal" symptoms.

Polk argues that just like the addict is indifferent, blind to the pain and suffering he causes in feeding his addiction, much of America's economic elite is similarly unconcerned by the social, economic distress being caused by the operation of neoliberal capitalism (the unregulated movement of capital worldwide). Indifference to the social effects of a profit-making regime is conveyed in the *Star Trek: Voyager* (1995-2001) episode "False Profits" (1996). A pair of Ferengi (Arridor and Kol) manipulate a planet's religious beliefs to install themselves as its leaders. Before the arrival of the Ferengis the native population (we are told) was "flourishing." Under the Ferengi's profit-making regime the Ferengi become very wealthy, and at the same time poverty proliferates

among the native population. ("The two Ferengi live in a palatial tem-
ple, while the people are lucky to have a roof over their heads.") Arridor
and Kol are completely inured to the suffering they've caused, only cel-
ebrating the wealth they've accumulated.

Another case of wealth addiction is portrayed in *Star Trek: The Next
Generation* (1987-1994) episode "The Neutral Zone" (1988). A capitalist,
Ralph Offenhouse, from the late 20th century is awoken from a cryo-
genic sleep in the 24th century. Immediately, Offenhouse's mind turns
to his money: "I have a substantial portfolio. It's critical I check on it."
Later, he adds, "I have to phone Geneva right away about my accounts.
The interest alone could be enough to buy even this ship." Subsequently,
Captain Picard informs Ralph that "a lot has changed in three hundred
years. People are no longer obsessed with the accumulation of 'things'.
We have eliminated hunger, want, the need for possessions. We have
grown out of our infancy." Ralph: "You've got it wrong. It's never been
about 'possessions' – it's about power." Significantly, Polk in his op-ed
piece holds that "Wall Street is a toxic culture that encourages the gran-
diosity of people who are desperately trying to feel powerful." Picard
asks Ralph: "Power to do what?"

> **Ralph:**   To control your life, your destiny.
> **Picard:** That kind of control is an illusion.

This notion of *controlling your life, your destiny* is particularly illusory in
a context where the planet is warming dangerously and the biosphere
is becoming de-stabilized as a result. Saliently, the wealth accumulation process is at the core of this planetary warming, de-stabilization.[46]
Again, like drug addicts, wealth addicts are inured to the immense
damage that their addiction causes others and themselves. The *Voyager*
episode "Future's End" (1996) features a technology capitalist (Ed
Starling) who in 1996 threatens to destroy Los Angeles and is mute to
the fact that his effort to travel into the future to bolster the fortunes of
his corporation will destroy the solar system in the 29th century.

---

46 George A. Gonzalez, *Urban Sprawl, Global Warming, and the Empire of Capital*
   (Albany: State University of New York Press, 2009); Jonathan Crary, *Scorched
   Earth: Beyond the Digital Age to a Post-Capitalist World* (New York: Verso, 2022).

Quark (also a Ferengi) travels back to mid-20th century Earth (more specifically, the United States), and concludes from his dealings with humans (Americans) in this epoch, that "these humans, they're not like the ones from the [24th century] Federation. They're crude, gullible and greedy" ("Little Green Men" 1995 – *Deep Space Nine*). Marx offers a consonant rebuke of the cultural/social ethos of capitalists: "Contempt for theory, art, history, and for man as an end in himself . . . is the real, conscious standpoint, the virtue of the man of money."[47] The former American President and long-time billionaire Donald J. Trump typifies the uncouth, anti-intellectual, even profane capitalist Marx identified over a century ago. Trump doesn't read.[48] He's a misogynist,[49] employs vulgar, coarse language in describing others,[50] and has openly associated himself with the pornography industry.[51]

The documentary *Born Rich* (2003) indicates that the scions of the extremely wealthy suffer from severe ennui – suggesting that a (neoliberalist) global society geared almost exclusively toward capital accumulation is misguided.[52] The unhappiness of capitalist elites is at the center of the television series *Mad Men* (2007–2015). Don Draper, the lead character, is at the top of the advertising industry during the Golden Age of the American economy – the 1950s into the mid-1960s. Draper philanders, smokes and drinks heavily to cope with the seeming emptiness of his life – ultimately leaving the business world and his wealth to join a commune.

---

47 Karl Marx, *On the Jewish Question*, 1844, http://www.marxists.org/archive/marx/works/1844/jewish-question/.

48 Katie Rogers, "Books Trump Can Praise Without Reading a Word," *New York Times*, Dec. 1, 2018, A18.

49 Billy Bush, "Yes, Donald Trump, You Said That," *New York Times*, Dec. 4, 2017, A21.

50 Kimon de Greef, and Sewell Chan, "Setback for U.S. Is Feared as Africa Recoils at Trump Remark," *New York Times*, Jan. 16, 2018, A8.

51 David Moye, "Donald Trump Appeared In A Playboy Softcore Porn Video," *Huffington Post*, Sept. 30, 2016. Web.

52 Adam Kotsko, *Neoliberalism's Demons: On the Political Theology of Late Capital* (Stanford: Stanford University Press, 2018).

Conclusion

The central argument in this volume is that art (especially popular culture) effectively communicates the methodology at the core of
the Hegel/Marx political philosophy paradigm. This methodology
is Mediation, Totality, Genesis, Praxis. As noted, these four components dialectically operate. The first position (or mediation) of Hegel/
Marx reasoning is that society is a totality – shaped by the Absolute.
Society and the Absolute interact (are dialectic) and for Marx a significant aspect of this dialectic is the means of production – the greater the
forces of production the greater the opportunities for universal justice.
Unfortunately, there are social forces intent on blocking/preventing the
advancement of society – despite the obvious perils of economic crisis, global warming and nuclear conflagration. A prime terrain of the
struggle between advancement and stasis (or the status quo) is popular
culture. This issue is treated in the next chapter.

Chapter Two

Praxis: Enlightenment versus the Anti-Enlightenment

What is the political content of the Enlightenment? Conversely, what does the anti-Enlightenment politically mean? The Enlightenment implies universal justice, fairness – but this is rather abstract. In practice the Enlightenment is social, political cohesion, solidarity – everyone working together to *elevate* the whole of humanity and achieve a sustainable, humane relationship with nature. Consonant with Hegel/ Marx, human universal solidarity is achieved through progressive revolutions. Interestingly, the creator of Star Trek, Gene Roddenberry, was very lucid about the evolutionary process of human social, political cohesion. Star Trek stands out in depicting revolutions whereby universal justice is progressively achieved – the basis of human solidarity. The anti-Enlightenment by implication implies disunity – people politically divided (everyone essentially fending for themselves).

Toward the end of his life Roddenberry gave an extended interview where he outlined a *telos* of human civilization that can be viewed as the unfolding *progressive dialectic* – whereby humanity is advancing toward an ideal endpoint of cohesion:

The usual way of the physical world is to progress towards unity. When life originated on this planet, it was a single-cell organism. And perhaps by accident, or need for survival, or some primal urge, these individual cells began to group together to form collectives, then units, then a corporate body. And that's what happens on a larger scale with humans. They form groups – tribes, nations, and so on. . . . If you follow the thought logically, you can project a more complex interaction – perhaps a thinking body in which the individual units no longer function in any capacity as individuals. They may specialize, but not without the knowledge and cooperation of the whole group. It's a kind of interdependence in which the whole is greater than the sum of its part.[1]

Roddenberry pointed to "computers" (science, technology) as an advancement toward human unity – drawing people together through increased information and communication flows. Thus, the original series was very optimistic about computers, even as they were a nascent technology in the late 1960s (when the original *Star Trek* was produced).[2]

Arguably, in the Star Trek franchise (its broadcast iterations) what can be observed is the praxis of the historic and ongoing *progressive dialectic* – beginning with the Stoic Turn and followed by the Socratic Turn. The Stoic Turn refers to the primacy of reason over emotion. The practical significance is it represents a rejection of superstition, the occult, the supernatural, and an embrace of empiricism.[3] The stoic turn in the world of Star Trek is fictionally salient with the Vulcans. Mr. Spock, a Vulcan and First-Officer of the Enterprise in the original series, notes that: "I prefer the concrete, the graspable, the provable" ("The Return of The Archons" 1967). According to the backstory of the Vulcans, they were an tensely emotional people and this resulted in continual violence ("All Our Yesterdays" 1969). The ancient teachings of Surak (*à la* Buddha or Jesus Christ)[4] brought about a planet-wide movement of

1 Yvonne Fern, *Gene Roddenberry: The Last Conversation* (Los Angeles: University of California Press, 1994), 16.

2 Ibid., 46. For a discussion of how computers, technology, information are the basis of a holistic, collective understanding of humanity and the natural world, see James Cheshire, and Oliver Uberti, *Atlas of the Invisible: Maps and Graphics That Will Change How You See the World* (New York: W. W. Norton, 2021).

3 John Sellars, *Stoicism* (Los Angeles: University of California Press, 2006).

4 Willard G. Oxtoby, Roy C. Amore, and Amir Hussain, *World Religions: Eastern Traditions*, 4th ed. (New York: Oxford University Press, 2014); C. Kavin Rowe, *One*

stoicism ("Savage Curtain" 1969). Mr. Spock's favorite phrase is (other than "fascinating") "logical", or conversely "illogical" – intuitively critiquing any supposition he deems outside of the empirical and/or reason. In the West, stoicism becomes particularly widespread with the establishment of Christianity as the official religion of the Roman Empire.[5] Christianity represents the overcoming of tribe/tribalism and the embrace of universalism – everyone (universally) is equal in the eyes of god.[6]

The Socratic Turn specifically refers to Socrates of ancient Greece.[7] Socrates is most famous for challenging the pagan theology and the-ocracy of ancient Athens. For this, he is executed. Socrates's defiance is artistically depicted in the original series episode of "Who Mourns for Adonis" (1967). The crew of the Enterprise comes across the god Apollo, who (along with the other gods of ancient Greek mythology) fled Earth when he ceased to be worshipped. Apollo captures the Enterprise with the hope of reviving humans' reverence for him. Captain Kirk defiantly informs Apollo that humans have *outgrown* their pagan beliefs (as well as superstitions) and now embrace monotheism – presumably a deist theology.[8] Kirk to Apollo: "Mankind has no need for gods. We find the one quite adequate."

While Socrates was a 4th century BCE figure, the Socratic Turn is part of the European Enlightenment of the 17th and 18th centuries. The Socratic Turn is specifically the demand that the state and politics reflect rationality.[9] This directly challenges the monarchical, aristocratic claim that a ruling caste has been ordained by God.[10] The Socratic Turn and

True Life: The Stoics and Early Christians as Rival Traditions (New Haven: Yale University Press, 2016).

5 Runar Thorsteinsson, *Roman Christianity and Roman Stoicism: A Comparative Study of Ancient Morality* (New York: Oxford University Press, 2013).

6 Morgan Rempel, *Nietzsche, Psychohistory, and the Birth of Christianity* (New York: Praeger, 2002).

7 Paul Johnson, *Socrates: A Man for Our Times* (New York: Penguin, 2012).

8 Jeffrey R. Wigelsworth, *Deism in Enlightenment England: Theology, Politics, and Newtonian Public Science* (Manchester: Manchester University Press, 2009).

9 Dustin Sebell, *The Socratic Turn: Knowledge of Good and Evil in an Age of Science* (Philadelphia: University of Pennsylvania Press, 2016).

10 Jonathan I. Israel, *Radical Enlightenment: Philosophy and the Making of Modernity, 1650–1750* (New York: Oxford University Press, 2001), and *Enlightenment*

the Enlightenment comes to a head with Thomas Paine's renowned pamphlet *Common Sense* (where he expressly mocks the idea of monarchy and aristocracy) and the American Revolution that was in significant part precipitated by this pamphlet. The affirmative rationality of the American Revolution is found in the phrase "all men are created equal."[11]

The Socratic Turn of the Enlightenment is in part portrayed in the original series episode "Omega Glory" (1968). It depicts a world with an identical history to that of Earth's, except in this instance the Cold War resulted in a globally devastating nuclear/biological war – where humans were reduced to a veritable stone age. Kirk ultimately realizes that the segment of the population that represented the West views the U.S. Constitution as a sacred document. But they cannot read it, so Kirk explains to them that it represents the Enlightenment concept of equality before the law: "That which you called Ee'd Plebnista was not written for chiefs or kings or warriors or the rich and powerful, but for all the people!" Kirk proceeds to read directly from this document (the Ee'd Plebnista), which is the Constitution:

> We the people of the United States, in order to form a more perfect union, establish justice, ensure domestic tranquillity, provide for the common defense, promote the general welfare, and secure the blessings of liberty to ourselves and our posterity ... do ordain and establish this constitution.

Asserting the revolutionary implications of the American Revolution and the Constitution that followed, Kirk declares "these words and the words that follow. . . They must apply to everyone or they mean nothing!"

The other significant aspect of the Enlightenment portrayed in the Star Trek text is the U.S. Civil War (1861-1865) – which resulted in the abolition of slavery (thereby serving to make "all men are created equal" more of a reality).[12] In "The Savage Curtain" (1969 – original series) the

Contested: Philosophy, Modernity, and the Emancipation of Man, 1670–1752 (New York: Oxford University Press, 2006).

11 Jonathan I. Israel, *The Expanding Blaze: How the American Revolution Ignited the World, 1775–1848* (Princeton: Princeton University Press, 2017).

12 Elizabeth R. Varon, *Disunion!: The Coming of the American Civil War, 1789–1859* (Chapel Hill: University of North Carolina Press, 2010).

Enterprise crew meets the incarnation of Abraham Lincoln. While acknowledging that this is not the real Lincoln, Kirk insists that the crew treat him with the respect and deference due this great historical figure – the leader of what many consider to be the second American Revolution (i.e., the victorious Northern Cause in the U.S. Civil War).[13] Kirk notes: "I cannot conceive it possible that Abraham Lincoln ... could have actually been reincarnated. And yet his kindness, his gentle wisdom, his humor, everything about him is so right." McCoy chides Kirk: "Practically the entire crew has seen you ... treat this impostor like the real thing ... when he can't possibly be the real article. Lincoln died three centuries ago hundreds of light-years away." Spock observes to Kirk: "President Lincoln has always been a very personal hero to you." Kirk retorts: "Not only to me." Spock: "Agreed."

To the American Revolutionary War and the U.S. Civil War, the Star Trek text adds to America's revolutionary "moments" with the Bell Uprising. Aired in 1995, the *Deep Space Nine* (1993-1999) episode "Past Tense" is centered on this fictional uprising. The characters Sisko, Bashir, and Dax are accidentally sent back to 2024 San Francisco. They encounter the San Francisco "Sanctuary District" – an urban zone where untold numbers of the poor and dispossessed are forcibly interned. "By the early twenty-twenties there was a place like this in every major city in the United States" – dirty, dilapidated, and overcrowded with "people without jobs or places to live." Sanctuary Districts are a metaphor for the de-industrialization, job loss, and disinvestment that major American urban areas[14] (such as Detroit[15] and Cleveland[16]) experienced

---

13 James M. McPherson, *Abraham Lincoln and the Second American Revolution* (New York: Oxford University Press, 1992); Gregory P. Downs, *The Second American Revolution: The Civil War-Era Struggle over Cuba and the Rebirth of the American Republic* (Chapel Hill: University of North Carolina Press, 2019).

14 Guin A. McKee, *The Problem of Jobs: Liberalism, Race, and Deindustrialization in Philadelphia* (Chicago: University of Chicago Press, 2009); Timothy Williams, "For Shrinking Cities, Destruction Is a Path to Renewal," *New York Times*, Nov. 12, 2013, A15; Jon Hurdle, "Philadelphia Forges Plan To Rebuild From Decay," *New York Times*, January 1, 2014, B1.

15 Thomas J. Sugrue, *The Origins of the Urban Crisis: Race and Inequality in Postwar Detroit* (Princeton: Princeton University Press, 2005); Joe Drape, "Bankruptcy for Ailing Detroit, but Prosperity for Its Teams," *New York Times*, Oct. 14., 2013, A1.

16 Carol Poh Miller, and Robert Wheeler, *Cleveland: A Concise History* (Bloomington: Indiana University Press, 2009).

as a result of neoliberal global capitalism[17] – with much of U.S. industry moving to cheaper labor venues.[18] "Past Tense" also refers to the tendency of technology to replace labor.[19] A Sanctuary District resident explains that "they laid a bunch of us off when they got some new equipment … and so I ended up here."

The overriding need to pursue humane politics/values is made clear in "Past Tense". Sisko inadvertently prevents the Bell Uprising. Like the victory of the Nazis in World War Two (*Star Trek*, original series – "City on the Edge of Forever" 1967), this erases the entire history of the Federation and chaos subsequently dominates Earth. Therefore, the failure of humanity to shift away from the current neoliberalism capitalist regime would result in societal collapse (the end of history). One is reminded of Rosa Luxemburg's pronouncement that the "future is either socialism or barbarism."[20]

Anti-Enlightenment

If the *progressive dialectic* (the Enlightenment) is increasing social/political solidarity/cohesion (as suggested by Roddenberry), then keeping people divided/segmented is the opposite (the anti-Enlightenment). One way to do so is to seek to entrench divisions among people through popular culture. American television and movies in the 1950s and 1960s can be viewed as sexist as well as racist. Racism was communicated through the absence of Afro actors/characters. The television series *Father Knows Best* (1954–1960) best typifies the sexism of postwar American popular culture. The civil rights, as well as the feminist,

---

17 Gérard Duménil, and Dominique Lévy, *Capital Resurgent: Roots of the Neoliberal Revolution*, trans. Derek Jeffers (Cambridge, MA: Harvard University Press, 2004).
18 Mary Elizabeth Gallagher, *Contagious Capitalism: Globalization and the Politics of Labor in China* (Princeton: Princeton University Press, 2005); David Koistinen, *Confronting Decline: The Political Economy of Deindustrialization in Twentieth-Century New England* (Gainesville: University Press of Florida, 2013).
19 James Steinhoff, *Automation and Autonomy: Labour, Capital and Machines in the Artificial Intelligence Industry* (New York: Palgrave Macmillan, 2021).
20 Stephen Eric Bronner, *Rosa Luxemburg: A Revolutionary for Our Times* (University Park: Pennsylvania State University Press, 1993).

movements fundamentally changed society and especially popular culture. Below I argue that Star Trek of the 1960s was at the center of social revolutions of the era. As a result of these revolutions women and ethnic minorities (including LGBTQ) are more fairly, equitably depicted in American popular culture.[21]

Nevertheless, the anti-Enlightenment is conveyed in popular culture through the idea that justice is not total. This is most clearly represented in what are known as *police shows*. Week in and week out crimes are committed and the police (through professionalism, humaneness, fairness) "get their man", and/or provide help to the people that need it. Shows like *Barney Miller* (1975–1982), *NYPD Blue* (1995–2005), *Blue Bloods* (2009 to present) depict police officers in idealized form – the way we'd like them to be. Setting aside the issue of whether such shows are "cop – a – ganda",[22] the more significant political aspect of police shows I would submit is that justice *in toto* is not possible. Instead justice is only possible on a piecemeal basis – one victim or one person in distress at a time.

The police show that appears to have the broadest political frame is *Blue Bloods*, as a central character is the New York City Police (NYPD) Commissioner – named Frank Reagan. As police chief his prime political concern is protecting the NYPD and its officers. At no point does Reagan advocate for directly addressing the causes of crimes and the social ills the police have to regularly deal with. Unemployment, poverty, economic insecurity, the lack of affordable housing and

---

21 Josh Ozersky, *Archie Bunker's America: TV in an Era of Change, 1968–1978* (Carbondale: Southern Illinois University Press, 2003); Samuel A. Chambers, *The Queer Politics of Television* (New York: I.B.Tauris, 2009); Judy Kutulas, *After Aquarius Dawned: How the Revolutions of the Sixties became the Popular Culture of the Seventies* (Chapel Hill: University of North Carolina Press, 2017).

22 Michael LaForgia, and Jennifer Valentino-DeVries, "Fabled Police Force Shows Limits of Death Inquiries," *New York Times*, Sept. 26, 2021, A1; Clay Risen, "Oris Buckner, Detective Who Blew Whistle on Police Abuse, Dies at 70," *New York Times*, June 9, 2022, B12; J. David Goodman, "Told of Injuries, Uvalde Police Still Hesitated," *New York Times*, June 10, 2022, A1, and "Response to Uvalde Shooting Called 'Abject Failure'," *New York Times*, June 22, 2022, A13; Shaila Dewan, "Flawed Autopsies Reflect Biases Even in Death," *New York Times*, June 21, 2022, A1.

adequate mental health facilities are issues that don't seemingly concern Commissioner Reagan.

The most saliently pessimistic and anti-Enlightenment of contemporary popular culture is the Star Wars franchise. Much of the action of the franchise centers on the "Force". The Force is explicitly anti-Enlightenment insofar as it is outside of rationality, science, and yet plays a central (political) role in society.

The franchise's pessimism is pronounced insofar as there is no social evolution, progress. Instead society is simply an unending cycle of stability and instability.[23] Metaphorically, in Star Wars this is represented in the alternating rulership between the *Jedi* and the *Sith*. The Jedi/Republic governed for ostensibly a significant number of years (prior to the rise of Empire led by Palpatine/Darth Vader), but it is not at all clear what this governance meant for the broader public. Noteworthy is the fact that under the *Galactic Republic* (Jedi governance) legal slavery is extant (the three prequel movies – *Phantom Menace* [1999], *Attack of the Clones* [2002], *Revenge of the Sith* [2005]). In the periphery (Tatooine) the great unwashed masses remain the great unwashed masses regardless of history, or circumstance. Thus, in a sense in the world of Star Wars there is no history – in terms of understanding the progress of social, political evolution. History in Star Wars is simply documenting which Jedi or Sith were politically dominant at any given time – otherwise society (and the masses) stay essentially the same over millennia.

What is glaringly missing from the Star Wars universe is any notion of justice. Those fighting the Empire (i.e., the Rebellion) saliently use the slogan "Freedom" – not "Justice". (There is no debate over the content of the galactic social order.) It's not clear why the average person would care whether the Empire or the Republic are in control? In the *Mandalorian* (2019–) Star Wars series ("The Believer" 2020) – commenting on the impoverished natives people on a planet, someone observes: "Empire, New Republic. It's all the same to these people."

---

23 Friedrich Nietzsche, *Beyond Good & Evil: Prelude to a Philosophy of the Future* (New York: Vintage,1989 [1886]); Beiner, *Dangerous Minds*; Wolin, *The Seduction of Unreason*.

What seemingly motives the struggle between the Jedi religious order and the Sith religious order is centralism versus regionalism. The Sith centralize political power in the galaxy (unitary government), whereby for the Republic democracy is equated with de-centralization (presumably confederacy, or at most federalism). For the Rebellion, *freedom* seemingly means freedom from central authority. President Ronald Reagan denounced the Soviet Union (the great centralizer of all authority) as the "Evil Empire"[24] because he favored the (radical) de-centralization of power/authority – both in terms of institutional governance (States' Rights) and economic decision-making (i.e., corporations).[25]

The nihilism and despair at the core of the anti-Enlightenment worldview is communicated in the recent Netflix iteration of the *Masters of the Universe* (2021). This animated franchise is fantasy and its free use of magic as a literary device makes it more kid's fare than philosophy. The Netflix series, however, does depict explicit philosophical pessimism and demoralization – consonant with anti-Enlightenment thinking. I'll note the Netflix iteration of *Masters of the Universe* is more adult in that the creators seek to explore issues of psychology and personal strife among its characters – including the use of sex to manipulate.

The premise of the franchise is philosophically enticing in that on its face it seeks to portray the *Absolute* – referred to as the "power of the universe". This points to the reality that the known universe is cosmos, not chaos – the laws of physics, the human intuitive sense of justice, fairness. The seeming order of the universe is found in this *power* and those that wield, protect it. The "power of the universe" (the basis of cosmos) emanates from Castle Grayskull. He-Man et al. are committed to shield it from those that would abuse this power. It is the villain

24 Francis X. Clines, "Reagan Denounces Ideology of Soviet as 'Focus of Evil'," *New York Times*, March 9, 1983. Web.
25 Jeffrey L. Chidester, and Paul Kengor, eds., *Reagan's Legacy in a World Transformed* (Cambridge, MA: Harvard University Press, 2015); Jonathan R. Hunt, and Simon Miles, eds., *The Reagan Moment: America and the World in the 1980s* (Ithaca: Cornell University Press, 2021).

of Skeletor and his henchmen that plot to seize Grayskull and use the *power of the universe* for their own ends.

In the 2021 Netflix season of *Masters of the Universe* Skeletor finally captures the sword that wields the power of the universe and Grayskull. Skeletor – now that he is able to become/understand the Whole – observes that:

> We want to believe in an ordered universe – some grand architecture holding it all together. But there is only *power* – beautiful, naked, chaotic *power!* And every so often, for some unfathomable reasons that power fixes itself to one person [formerly He-Man and now Skeletor]. *One in all creation!* ("Cleaved in the Twain" 2021)

Put differently, there is no telos to the universe, no inherent justice, fairness. In the end the universe is chaos save for the person that controls its *power*. This, in a sense, encapsulates the anti-Enlightenment position. Social order is purely a function of (state) power and those that wield it – there is no inherent (metaphysical) justice at the core of politics, society.

This conclusion sends Skeletor's accomplice, Evil-lyn, into an emotional tailspin. The audience learns of Evil-lyn's hardscrabble upbringing. She was born into extreme poverty, and as a child had to run away from home because her parents were so impoverished that they decided to literally eat Evil-lyn to survive. Growing up on the streets she had to endure abuse. After 20 years of this existence Skeletor *rescues* her ("Gutter Rat" 2021). Skeletor, however, is verbally, physically abusive and regularly spews vitriol to those around him. Evil-lyn ultimately succeeds in taking the sword from Skeletor (using sex as a ruse) that wields the *power of the universe* and with it is determined to destroy all of creation. Evil-lyn decides to end the universe because anguish and suffering serves no broader purpose and will continue *ad infinitum*: "It's all just so empty. There's no design, so there's no meaning. *It's all just pain*" ("Gutter Rat").

Conclusion

The Star Trek creators (Roddenberry among them) engage in Enlightenment philosophy – artistically depicting key instances when humanity collectively overcame backwardness (obscurantism, injustice), as well as speculating on future progressive revolutions. This is the embodiment of praxis insofar as Star Trek inspires us toward collective, worldwide justice (solidarity) – the *elevation* of humanity.[26] "In the Cards" (1997 – *Deep Space Nine*), the point is explicitly, optimistically made that in the future society will be based on a "philosophy of *self-enhancement* [. . .] We work to better ourselves and the rest of Humanity."

Through its portrayal via popular culture it is evident that the anti-Enlightenment is not philosophy, but a pessimistic politics. It offers little more than the dim view that collective justice (solidarity) is not on the agenda, and as a result mass suffering and victimization are eternal aspects of human existence. The best anyone can hope for is that individually we do not fall prey to poverty, violence, discrimination, etc.

---

26 David Estlund, *Utopophobia: On the Limits (If Any) of Political Philosophy* (Princeton: Princeton University Press, 2019).

Chapter Three

Star Trek (Original Series) Against Patriarchy and Jim Crow

The 1950s was a particularly repressive period in U.S. history. This was the height of the anti-communist hysteria.[1] With anti-communism came a resurgence of white supremacy[2] and rigid patriarchy.[3] As a result (along with the repression of dissent), minorities suffered greatly – women, gays, lesbians, African Americans, etc. experienced dramatic setbacks. The regressiveness of this period is arguably most emblematic with the 1950s television series *Father Knows Best*. The overt implication is that the official family of the U.S. (at the height of its global power) is white; unquestioning of corporate or American power; heterosexual; with the male (father) as head of household. The father is due the deference of the family – who will represent the family in the public sphere and select the life course of his children (remember, Father Knows

---

1   David M. Oshinsky, *A Conspiracy So Immense: The World of Joe McCarthy* (New York: Oxford University Press, 2005); Christopher M. Elias, *Gossip Men: J. Edgar Hoover, Joe McCarthy, Roy Cohn, and the Politics of Insinuation* (Chicago: University of Chicago Press, 2021).

2   Editorial Board, "Why Does the U.S. Military Celebrate White Supremacy?" *New York Times*, May 24, 2020, SR8.

3   Gerda Lerner, *The Creation of Patriarchy* (New York: Oxford University Press, 1986).

Best!). The duty of women is to marry, have and nurture children, and, importantly, submit to her husband's authority (as well as uphold it).[4]

My argument in this chapter is that the *Star Trek* television series of the 1960s presented a uniquely strong stance in favor of the Enlightenment – denouncing the discrimination and oppression that women and African Americans experienced during this period. Thus, the creators of *Star Trek* were not simply conveying, commenting on the Enlightenment politics of its day, they were direct participants in advocating for it. *Star Trek* episodes "Elaan of Troyius" (1968) and "Turnabout Intruder" (1969) present female characters openly, unambiguously, stridently railing against the sexism of the times. Moreover, *Star Trek* presented a future with a world government, and total ethnic equality – including the hero worship of Abraham Lincoln (episode "Savage Curtain" [1969]). "Let that Be your Last Battlefield" (1969) directly critiques the racial hate of the Jim Crow South. The use of racism to prop up a profoundly unjust social order is depicted in "The Cloud Minders" (1969) and the creators of "Day of the Dove" (1968) denounce the use of racism by anti-communists. I begin the analysis by outlining the anti-sexism of original series *Star Trek*, and follow this by describing its anti-racism.

---

4   Marilyn Yalom, *A History of the Wife* (New York: HarperCollins, 2001); Stephanie Coontz, *Marriage, a History: From Obedience to Intimacy, or How Love Conquered Marriage* (New York: Viking, 2005).

Star Trek as Feminist Tract

The liberal feminist[5] movement of the 1960s helped undue much of the repression that women experienced in the 1950s.[6] *Star Trek* can be deemed as a salient part of this movement as it is distinct from what can be deemed feminist television in the late 1960s and early 1970s. Shows like *Julia* (1968–1971) and *Mary Tyler Moore* (1970–1977) depict single women successfully making their way in the world, but they stayed clear of bemoaning the systematic, debilitating, frustrating discrimination (oppression) that women faced.[7] *Star Trek* stands out on this score.

David Greven, in *Gender and Sexuality in Star Trek*, holds that the bold progressiveness of *Star Trek* (original series) in the realms of gender and queer politics is that marriage and biological family play only a minimal role in the series.[8] Instead, *Star Trek* features individuals that find meaningful fellowship, emotional intimacy among co-workers, friends. On the question of gender, the regular character of Lt. Uhura is noteworthy – she's a career woman and a bridge officer. With regard to homosexuality, Star Trek of the 1960s had no gay or lesbian characters, but, significantly, the series had what can be deemed the gayest moment of American television (certainly up until that time). In "Turnabout Intruder" (described in more detail below) Captain Kirk's body is taken over by a woman. Her/his co-conspirator is a male, who she apparently manipulated with sex. While in Kirk's body, this character uses her feminine charms on her accomplice – pulling up behind him, gently placing his hand on his shoulder, and speaking to him in a seductive tone. He complies with her/his request.

---

5   Kimberly Wilmot Voss, *Women Politicking Politely: Advancing Feminism in the 1960s and 1970s* (Lanham, MD: Lexington Books, 2017).
6   Editors of LIFE, *LIFE The 1960s: The Decade When Everything Changed* (New York: LIFE, 2016); Henry Finder, ed., *The 60s: The Story of a Decade* (New York: New Yorker, 2016); Editors of History Channel, *History The 1960's* (New York: History Channel, 2019).
7   Josh Ozersky, *Archie Bunker's America: TV in an Era of Change, 1968–1978* (Carbondale: Southern Illinois University Press, 2003); Judy Kutulas, *After Aquarius Dawned: How the Revolutions of the Sixties became the Popular Culture of the Seventies* (Chapel Hill: University of North Carolina Press, 2017), chap. 3.
8   David Greven, *Gender and Sexuality in Star Trek: Allegories of Desire in the Television Series and Films* (Jefferson, NC: MacFarland, 2009).

Women as Strong

Daniel Leonard Bernardi, in *Star Trek and History: Race-ing toward a White Future*, takes an ahistorical tack and denounces the fact that the character of Lt. Uhura was a supporting role.[9] The disparaging of the Uhura character ignores the great importance of having a bridge officer on the Enterprise in the late 1960s that is a female (and African American). Regardless of the content of the role, the character of Uhura on the bridge of the Enterprise week in and week out glaringly communicated that the future of humanity was one of ethnic, gender equality.

Moreover, women in the original series play autonomous, assertive characters – including that of a Romulan ship captain, who has male subordinates ("The Enterprise Incident" 1968). "Time Amok" (1967) has Mr. Spock's betrothed scheming to escape their arranged marriage. A young woman in "Cloud Minders" eschews a life of comfort and opulence to live among the poor, destitute of her planet. "Day of the Dove" features a woman as a Klingon science officer, who breaks with her commanding officer (also her husband) – holding that Kirk *et al.* possess the correct understanding of the situation facing both the Klingon and Enterprise crews. The Elaan, Dohlman of Elas, is an (aristocratic) political leader – the men in her entourage kneel before her. She prioritizes strategic thinking: "We are interested in how the ship is used in combat, not in what drives it. Engines are for mechanics and menials" ("Elaan of Troyius"). "Wink of an Eye" (1968) features a woman leader of a group seeking to take over the Enterprise. She asserts her sexuality – kissing Captain Kirk (trying to seduce him) and calling him "pretty." Similarly, Elaan tells Captain Kirk "I chose you." "Court Martial" (1967) has a female lead prosecutor.

The character of Edith Keeler in "City on the Edge of Forever" (1967) is particularly significant as a feminist figure in the later 1960s. David Greven, in his outstanding book *Gender and Sexuality in Star Trek*, makes the effective argument that Kirk's trysts were mostly cast as exotic and extraneous.[10] The one exception to this is Kirk's relationship with Keeler.

9   Daniel Leonard Bernardi, *Star Trek and History: Race-ing toward a White Future* (New Brunswick, NJ: Rutgers University Press, 1998).
10 Greven, *Gender and Sexuality in Star Trek*.

Keeler committed her life to helping the poor, as she "runs" the "21st Street Mission" – an organization, venue giving aid to the economically displaced. With Kirk and Spock down and out in New York City during the Great Depression of the 1930s, Keeler's kindness, charity, and idealism render her very endearing and attractive to the audience as a well as to Kirk. Kirk and Keeler share the same social justice values of the 1960s counterculture (including an anti-war outlook):

Keeler: I think that one day they'll take all the money they spend now on war and death . . .

Kirk: And make them spend it on life?

Keeler: Yes. You see the same things that I do. We speak the same language.

Kirk: The very same.

In another scene, Keeler speechifies optimistically to a group of homeless about a future without poverty, where all can thrive:

The days and the years ahead are worth living for. One day soon man is going to be able to harness incredible energies, maybe even the atom. Energies that could ultimately hurl us to other worlds in some sort of spaceship. And the men that reach out into space will be able to find ways to feed the hungry millions of the world and to cure their diseases. They will be able to find a way to give each man hope and a common future, and those are the days worth living for. Our deserts will bloom.

This vision (of technological advancement serving the ends of social justice) is consonant with FDR's New Deal of the 1930s[11] – Roosevelt being reverentially invoked in the episode. Keeler's autonomy, leadership, and political awareness makes her an iconic figure of 1960s feminism – especially considering the countless times that the episode "City on the Edge of Forever" has been broadcast around the world.

---

11 Kenneth J. Bindas, *Modernity and the Great Depression: The Transformation of American Society, 1930–1941* (Lawrence: University Press of Kansas, 2017).

Women as Second Class Citizens

Importantly, while positing an image of women as autonomous and assertive, *Star Trek* directly confronts the hardships that they endure. For instance, unlike men, women at the time had to mostly choose between career or family. "The Man Trap" (1966) did feature a husband and wife archaeological team, but, conversely, Lt. Uhura is unmarried and childless. Episode "Is There In Truth No Beauty?" (1968) centers on a female character who places career above romantic entanglement. When she refuses her suitor he chides her by questioning her womanhood: "Why don't you try being a woman for a change?" Captain Kirk's former lover rebukes him for choosing Starfleet (exploring space) over a relationship with her. He indicates that she's too strong willed: "We'd have killed each other" ("Turnabout Intruder").

Elaan, Dohlman of Elas, is a metaphor for the pressure that women face to marry, and that they're expected to demure to their husbands (i.e., to be lady-like) ("Elaan of Troyius"). She is livid that she's being forced to marry the ruler of Troyius. The Ambassador of Troyius: "Our two warring planets now possess the capability of mutual destruction. Some method of co-existence must be found." Elaan: "I will never forgive the council for putting me through this torture." She brutally stabs the Ambassador of Troyius because he expected that she "adopt . . . servile manners" – that is, conform to traditional female etiquette. Elaan ruefully notes: "That's all you men . . . can speak of, duty and responsibility." She concludes that as a woman "I have only responsibilities and obligations," and, conversely, no freedom – as she's being forced to marry and kowtow to her husband.

Captain Kirk (in response to Elaan's obstreperous behavior): "Mister Spock, the women on your planet are logical. That's the only planet in this galaxy that can make that claim." Of course, this claim can be read as sexist. A broader read is that women shouldn't be pigeonholed into the institution of marriage. Women, like men, are inherently unpredictable (that is, illogical), each with their own unique hopes, dreams, aspirations. Nor should women be forced into traditional female etiquette – which demands a woman be genteel, demure.[12] Women are

---

12 Kim E. Nielsen, *Money, Marriage, and Madness: The Life of Anna Ott* (Urbana: University of Illinois Press, 2020).

especially expected to be emotionally self-contained, reserved in pub-lic.[13] "Logic" for men and women is different, and skewed against women openly (unabashedly) expressing anger, displeasure, desire, ambition, etc. Elaan (with her "illogical" behavior) – angry shouting; making unreasonable demands; acting out by breaking objects – is an ironic metaphor of the oppressive strictures that women have to endure.

The creators of *Star Trek* take specific aim at the conservative (mis) treatment of women. A metaphor for Saudi Arabia is depicted in "Friday's Child" (1967) – while not veiled, the women dress in the man-ner redolent of the traditional Middle East. The planet Capella Four is governed by the Ten Tribes and a rigid patriarchy where honor kill-ings (protecting the *honor* of the family) are the norm: "You touch it [a piece of food being offered by a woman], her nearest male relative will have to try to kill you." When the top tribal leader is killed, his young wife (who is pregnant) is duty bound to kill herself. Like Saudi Arabia, Capella Four is of great strategic importance because of its min-eral wealth: "The rare mineral topaline, vital to the life-support sys-tems of planetoid colonies, has been discovered in abundance here." Additionally, "Mudd's Women" (1966) highlights the historic practice of sending women to the frontier for purposes of matching them with a husband.[14] Harvey Mudd traffics women to wealthy men that mine precious minerals on barren, forbidding planets.

"Turnabout Intruder" is distinct in American popular culture for its glaring critique of the discrimination that women faced at the time. The prejudices that women face on a regular basis have driven Janice Lester insane. It is observed that "Janice has driven herself mad with jealousy, hatred and ambition" – ostensibly because society placed arti-ficial, arbitrary (maddening) limits upon her.

While on "Camus Two . . . exploring the ruins of a dead civiliza-tion", Lester had almost her entire scientific team murdered and is feigning illness. She has manufactured a crisis to lure Captain Kirk

13 Laura Claridge, *Emily Post: Daughter of the Gilded Age, Mistress of American Manners* (New York: Random House, 2009); Ted Ownby, ed., *Manners and Southern History* (Jackson: University Press of Mississippi, 2011).
14 Albert L. Hurtado, *Intimate Frontiers: Sex, Gender, and Culture in Old California* (Albuquerque: University of New Mexico Press, 1999).

into a trap. Lester has discovered an ancient device that allows her to switch her consciousness with that of Captain Kirk – a former lover. Kirk says he had to break it off the romantic relationship with Lester because she holds "intense hatred of her own womanhood." Lester is "alone" (unmarried) because of her ambitions, but they are unfulfilled precisely because she is a woman. Upon executing her plan and taking over Kirk's body, she declares to him (in Lester's body): "Now you know the indignity of being a woman . . . it's better to be dead than to live alone in the body of a woman. It's better to be dead."

Lester says of Kirk: "I love the life he led. The *power* of a starship commander." Lester denounces the discrimination (unfairness) that women experienced at the time: "Your world of starship captains doesn't admit women. It isn't fair." The lead character, Mary Richards, of the *Mary Tyler Moore Show* was promoted from "Associate Producer" to "Producer" of the evening news for a local television station. The character, however, was not ambitious nor confrontational about (un) equal opportunities in the workplace.[15]

The Sexual Revolution on Television

Star Trek of the 1960s was a prominent vehicle of feminism in part because female characters dressed provocatively – i.e., they controlled and displayed their sexuality. The liability of such sartorial choices is that women become objectified – that is, judged solely based on their physical appearance, attributes. Thus, *Star Trek* helped to initiate the phenomenon of the 1970s television female sex symbol.[16] A farsighted, prescient critique of this phenomenon, Captain Kirk observes that "most of us are attracted by beauty and repelled by ugliness. *One of the last of our prejudices*" ("Is There In Truth No Beauty?"). In "Mudd's Women" the superficiality of pulchritude is critiqued – as a drug is used to make women physically beautiful ("It's not real!"). Indicating

---

15 Kutulas, *After Aquarius Dawned*, 95–96.
16 Elana Levine, *Wallowing in Sex: The New Sexual Culture of 1970s American Television* (Durham: Duke University Press, 2007), chap. 4.

that true beauty only comes from within, Kirk asserts that "You either believe in yourself, or you don't."

Elana Levine, in *Wallowing in Sex: The New Sexual Culture of 1970s American Television*, observes that as sex became more openly discussed, treated in popular culture (as a result of the 1960s) a wave of 1970s and early 1980s television movies portrayed children, teenagers as being sexually endangered, exploited, abused. She holds these movies were a conservative backlash to the new openness surrounding sex. The idea being that young people would be drawn (vulnerable) to dangerous sexual circumstances as a result of its portrayal on television.[17]

Star Trek of the 1960s contributed toward the libertine attitudes that would free society from the puritanism of the 1950s.[18] As noted, the women's attire in the series verged on the scandalous – even by today's standards (with female officers, for instance, sporting mini-skirts). Kirk had a number of sexual trysts – often peripheral to the main plot.[19] The sexuality of other characters was frequently on display. Spock's desire for sex was the prime theme of the episode "Time Amok". "Cloud Minders" has a young woman and Spock demonstrating mutual romantic attraction. "This Side of Paradise" (1967) has Spock spending his days lounging around in a bucolic setting with a beautiful young woman. Additionally, in the "The Enterprise Incident" Spock and the female Romulan ship captain engage in heavy petting – clearly manifesting sexual arousal. Despite the fact that he is older, Doctor McCoy is an incurable flirt. In "Mudd's Women" the men on the Enterprise are openly desirous of three women who take drugs to appear especially attractive.

Taking Levine's argument in *Wallowing in Sex* as valid: the bevy of child/teenage endangerment movies of the 1970s were a conservative critique of the new sexual openness. What popular culture mostly ignored was the danger that children and women were in under the gender regime of the conservative 1950s. "Friday's Child" is an

---

17 Levine, *Wallowing in Sex*, chap. 3.
18 Stephen R. Duncan, *The Rebel Café: Sex, Race, and Politics in Cold War America's Nightclub Underground* (Baltimore: Johns Hopkins University Press, 2018).
19 Greven, *Gender and Sexuality*.

unambiguous commentary on the fact that under conservative political values women's lives are deemed to have less value than those of
men. Historically, women were treated as currency – as indicated in
"Mudd's Women" (where women are "sold" to wealthy frontier husbands). "Bread and Circuses" (1968) – Kirk (on "a conservative world
based on time-honoured … strengths and virtues") is provided a slave
for his sexual pleasure.

The norms of privacy and patriarchy create an ideal circumstance
for mistreatment. The fact that young couples were pressed and forced
to marry (as highlighted in "Elaan of Troyius") could/would create
frustration for men that could result in the physical abuse of women
and children. "Requiem for Methuselah" (1969) suggests incest as a
recluse is in love with a young woman (android) he created.

If, indeed, teenagers running away became a salient phenomenon
in the 1970s (as suggested by the movies Levine outlines), a factor that is
not explored in these television movies is the friction created between
parents (who hewed to the politics and values of the 1950s) and the 1960s
generation. "The Way to Eden" (1969) features a group of mostly young
hippie types who are disdainful of official institutions ("We recognize
no authority") for their putative corruption (medicine is "the product
of prejudice, not science") and racism: referring to Captain Kirk as the
"great white captain." The rebellious group uses the phrase "Herbert"
as an epithet: "a minor official notorious for his rigid and limited patterns of thought." The group is estranged from their parents – "think
young" is one of their slogans.

Anti-Racism

The television series Star Trek was a salient victory for the U.S. civil
rights movement of the 1960s,[20] and arguably played a key role in end-
ing the open, official proclamation of white supremacy in the American

---

20 Bruce J. Dierenfield, *The Civil Rights Movement*, rev. ed. (New York: Routledge, 2014);
    George A. Gonzalez, "'May we Together Become Greater'": in Defence of Star Trek
    and Anti-Racism," *Foundation: The International Review of Science Fiction* 50, no. 138
    (2021): 14-22.

South.[21] The series aired when the civil rights movement was being attacked as part of a global communist conspiracy and the practice of lynching was still alive.[22]

Somewhat surprisingly, however, *Star Trek* (the original series) is cast as unfair to ethnic minorities – including African Americans. André M. Carrington, in *Speculative Blackness: The Future of Race in Science Fiction*, stands out on this score.[23] Carrington takes an ahistorical tack and denounces the fact that the character of Lt. Uhura (the one African-American bridge officer in the original series) was a supporting role. (Bernardi also assails the fact that Klingons are dark-skinned. I discuss this below.[24]) The significance of Uhura to the civil rights movement of the era is indicated by the fact that according to Nichelle Nichols (who played Uhura) when she was thinking of leaving the series no less than Martin Luther King, Jr. asked her to continue on the show.[25] It is also noteworthy that in "The Ultimate Computer" (1968) an African American plays one of the leading minds of the Federation, and in the episode "Court Martial" an American African is cast as an admiral. All are a direct rejection (mocking) of the white supremacy that was prevalent in the U.S. South at the time – as indicated by the fact that the rabidly racist/segregationist George Wallace won five Deep South states in the presidential election of 1968.[26]

A clear rejection of ethnic bigotry ("whitism") is portrayed by Captain Kirk and First Officer Spock (a Vulcan) in "Whom Gods Destroy" (1969). Kirk speaks of the founders of the Federation: "They

21 Adam H. Domby, *The False Cause: Fraud, Fabrication, and White Supremacy in Confederate Memory* (Charlottesville: University of Virginia Press, 2020).
22 M. J. Heale, *McCarthy's Americans: Red Scare Politics in State and Nation, 1935–1965* (Athens: University of Georgia Press, 1998); Jeff Woods, *Black Struggle, Red Scare: Segregation and Anti-Communism in the South, 1948–1968* (Baton Rouge: Louisiana State University, 2004).
23 André M. Carrington, *Speculative Blackness: The Future of Race in Science Fiction* (Minneapolis: University of Minnesota Press, 2016).
24 Bernardi, *Star Trek and History.*
25 Nichelle Nichols, *Beyond Uhura – Star Trek and Other Memories* (New York: G. P. Putnam's Sons, 1994), 164–65.
26 Dan T. Carter, *The Politics of Rage: George Wallace, the Origins of the New Conservatism, and the Transformation of American Politics*, 2nd ed. (Baton Rouge: Louisiana State University, 2000).

were humanitarians and statesmen, and they had a dream. A dream that became a reality and spread throughout the stars, a dream that made Mister Spock and me brothers." Indicative of how the Federation transcends all ethnic, religious and species divisions, Spock, when asked "do you consider Captain Kirk and yourself brothers?", replies: "Captain Kirk speaks somewhat figuratively and with undue emotion. However, what he says is logical and I do, in fact, agree with it."

In "Court Martial" Captain Kirk is tried by a multi-ethnic panel of four officers – one member with an Afro background and another with a central Asian background. At the opening of the proceedings, Kirk is asked "if you feel that any of these [individuals] harbor any prejudiced attitudes to your case"? – as Kirk has the "right to ask for substitute officers." Kirk: "I have no objections" – firmly believing that ethnicity (nor gender – the female prosecutor) will have any bearing whatsoever on the trial that will determine his fate. An affirmative nod to the civil rights movement is found in the Star Trek portrayal of Abraham Lincoln – the "Great Emancipator".[27]

Abraham Lincoln the Great Emancipator

Lincoln before Lincoln by Brian J. Snee is a survey, analysis of broadcast treatments of Abraham Lincoln prior to Steven Spielberg's 2012 movie *Lincoln*. Snee's most significant finding is that prior to Spielberg's movie, Lincoln as *Great Emancipator* is underplayed, if not totally ignored, in the numerous cinematic and television representations of the 16th U.S. President. Snee explains that "Beginning with D. W. Griffith's *The Birth of a Nation*—an overtly racist film that laments the demise of the Confederacy and celebrates the formation of the Ku Klux Klan— Hollywood routinely minimized or simply ignored Lincoln's role as the emancipator."[28]

27 James M. McPherson, *Abraham Lincoln and the Second American Revolution* (New York: Oxford University Press, 1992); Gregory P. Downs, *The Second American Revolution: The Civil War-Era Struggle over Cuba and the Rebirth of the American Republic* (Chapel Hill: University of North Carolina Press, 2019).
28 Brian J. Snee, *Lincoln before* Lincoln (Lexington: University of Kentucky Press, 2016), 25.

Snee unduly overlooks the treatment that Lincoln received in the episode "Savage Curtain". Snee only writes about Lincoln's appearance in "Savage Curtain" that it was "absurdly creative."[29] Star Trek's Lincoln is arguably the most important popular culture representation of the man as the franchise is ostensibly the most popular in U.S. television history – and "Savage Curtain" has been replayed literally innumerable (or countless) times worldwide. Unlike other television and movie portrayals of Lincoln (outside of Spielberg's *Lincoln*), Star Trek's creators convey him as a figure of immense historic, global importance. Lincoln's portrayal in "Savage Curtain" serves the overall globalist (anti-racist) outlook evident in the *Star Trek* original series.[30] In *Star Trek* Lincoln is cast as a figure that forwarded progressive modernism – on a worldwide basis.[31]

Lincoln comes to life in "Savage Curtain" because an alien race that the starship Enterprise has newly come into contact with wants to learn about good and evil – ideas that are foreign to them. The aliens create figures from the past of the Federation (an interstellar organization encompassing Earth) – Lincoln being one of them. The camps designated "good" and "evil" ultimately fight it out in an experiment to learn about these concepts. Lincoln is in the camp representing good.

While Lincoln was an American President, as the leader of the Northern victory over the Southern slavocracy he is a figure of worldwide saliency.[32] Arguably, Lincoln is the person most credited in the modern era with the defeat of feudalism in the West, and the concomitant triumph of progressive modernism.[33] The editors of the volume

---

29 Ibid., 22.
30 George A. Gonzalez, *Star Trek and the Politics of Globalism* (New York: Palgrave Macmillan, 2018).
31 Modernism is a set of normative values that privileges reason and secularism, as opposed to obscurantism and political religion (i.e., theocracy). Roland Vegso, *The Naked Communist: Cold War Modernism and the Politics of Popular Culture* (New York: Fordham University Press, 2013); Peter Childs, *Modernism*, 3rd ed. (New York: Routledge, 2016).
32 Downs, *The Second American Revolution*.
33 See note #31 of this chapter.

The Global Lincoln explain that "Lincoln's global celebrity lies in . . . his resolute defense of popular government and free labor."[34]

Of the avatars created to conduct the aliens' experiment, Lincoln (by far) receives the most attention – as he is a guest abroad Enterprise (whereas the others are not). Significantly, (as discussed in Chapter Two) James T. Kirk (captain of the Enterprise) in the 23rd century strongly admires the personage of Lincoln, so much so that Kirk shows great deference and respect to what is obviously an ersatz Lincoln. The fact that Kirk (and others) would admire Lincoln 300 years after his death and in a context of world government (i.e., the U.S. no longer exists) in-and-itself indicates that Lincoln is a figure of substantial historic and global importance.

Importantly, other than Lincoln on the "good" team is Surak – a Vulcan. He is cast as a modernizing figure for the Vulcans. Spock (a Vulcan) on Surak: "The greatest of all who ever lived on our planet. The father of all we became." Hence, Lincoln and Surak (who are teamed together along with Kirk and Spock) mirror each other – as both were world changing figures for their respective planets.

With the characters of Uhura and Lincoln, the creators of *Star Trek* are directly, unambiguously defying/challenging the Jim Crow South. The episode "Let that Be Your Last Battlefield" is an explicit and pointed critique, rejection of Southern race hatred.

An Anti-Jim Crow Polemic

Perhaps what is most glaring in Bernardi's and Carrington's treatment of the identity politics of the Star Trek franchise is the fact that neither make any comment on the original series episode "Let That Be Your Last Battlefield" – an episode that is explicitly anti-racist. The Enterprise crew comes into contact with an alien race that is half white and half black, but part of the population is white on the right side and the other is white on the left side. The Enterprise crew cannot fathom that such a trivial difference would be politically, socially significant

---

34 Richard Carwardine, and Jay Sexton, eds., *The Global Lincoln* (New York: Oxford University Press, 2011), ix.

for anyone – much less fuel the intense hatred and violence that the two alien individuals on-board the Enterprise (Lokai and Bele) direct toward one another (each one from the different ethnic groups).

Most significantly, the alien characters replicate the debate surrounding the 1960s civil rights movement – including *race supremacy*. The member of the oppressed caste reprises the history of Southern slavery – Lokai: they "tore us from our families, herded us together like cattle and then sold us as slaves!" The representative of the dominant group conveys the condescension, paternalism of the Southern Lost Cause false narrative – Bele: "They were savages . . . We took them into our hearts, our homes." Bele continues: "Slaves? . . . You were freed." Ostensibly referring to the conditions of the Jim Crow South, Lokai: "Freed? Were we free to be men? Free to be husbands and fathers? Free to live our lives in equality and dignity?" Overtly defending race-based casteism – Bele: "There is an order in things [...] It is obvious to the most simpleminded that Lokai is of an inferior breed." Lokai, later speaking to the Enterprise crew, asks them (really, the audience) to empathize with the profound injustice and wanton violence that people of his ethnicity (really, African Americans) experience:

> How can you understand my fear, my apprehension, my degradation, my suffering? . . . How can I make your flesh know how it feels to see all those who are like you, and only because they are like you, despised, slaughtered, and even worse, denied the simplest bit of decency that is a living being's right?

In the end we learn that the racism of this civilization resulted in its destruction.

It is significant that in the denouement of the episode Uhura proclaims that the behavior of these aliens "doesn't make any sense." She resides in a world of ethnic equality and fairness and cannot understand how people could hate so profoundly over something like skin tone. Spock, a Vulcan who works among humans, is similarly incredulous: "To expect sense from two mentalities of such extreme viewpoints is not logical." The point is made by the Enterprise crew that "There was persecution on Earth once [. . .] but it happened way back in the twentieth century. There's no such primitive thinking today." The future is ethnic equality and a rejection of race casteism as *primitive thinking.*

The original series episode "Cloud Minders" (as outlined in Chapter One) depicts a society (the planet of Ardana) where torture technology ("the rays") and racism are used to maintain/stabilize a caste system. The leader of Adrana, in justifying the use of torture, spews overt racism: Troglytes are "a conglomerate of inferior species." Enterprise's Doctor McCoy, in referring to Adrana's leader and the fact that race hatred is politically, intellectually (morally) blinding, dryly notes, "It's pretty hard to overcome prejudice."

Racism was deployed to unite the American public in fighting the Cold War. In the original series episode "Day of the Dove" an alien is surreptitiously fostering animosity between the Enterprise crew and Klingons on broad – including promoting "race hatred".

The Klingons and the Cold War

As noted above, Bernardi finds fault with the fact that the prime adversaries of the Federation (in the original series) are the dark-skinned Klingons. The Klingons utilize torture technology ("Day of the Dove") and engage in brutal collective punishment – executing groups of subject peoples for transgressions by individuals ("Errand of Mercy" 1967). Nevertheless, it is the height of cynicism to hold that the creators of Star Trek are making a regressive, hateful commentary by giving the Klingons dark-skin. A similar observation can be made of the critiques of the Uhura character. The number of lines assigned to Uhura, like the skin tone of the Klingons, can be reasonably interpreted as artistic choices – not politically motivated ones.

If one were to read politics into the skin-tone of the Klingons during the original series, the darker hue of the enemy of the Federation could be aptly viewed as an overt effort to avoid having the Klingons viewed as a metaphor for the Soviet Union. The field of *Star Trek Studies* has been maligned by two hugely flawed assumptions: (1) that the original series is a metaphor for the Cold War (professor of U.S. television history, Rick Worland: "the Klingons and the Federation were firmly established as two ideologically opposed superpower blocs"[35]), and, even more egregious, (2) that the Federation represents a kind of pro-American political trope (professor of international relations, Mark P. Lagon: "the zealous desire of James T. Kirk, as the hero of the original *Star Trek*, to spread the Federation's way of life serves as a mirror to observe the American style of foreign policy"[36]). (English professor, M. Keith Booker: Captain "Kirk is a walking icon of Americanism."[37]) These misplaced assumptions have worked to de-value *Star Trek* as pro-American Cold War propaganda. A particular strike against the idea that the original *Star Trek* can be reduced to a metaphor of the Cold War is that there is nothing Soviet/Russian about the Klingons[38] – including the way they look.

Star Trek is not a metaphor of the Cold War, but a commentary on great power politics of the era. The original series can be interpreted as offering a critical stance on the West's (U.S.'s) conduct in its competition with the Soviet Union. In the episode "Arena" (1967) it is acknowledged that the West engages in aggressive, militaristic colonization. A Federation colony in a remote region of space is attacked and Kirk is determined to destroy the offending ship to make an example of it:

Spock: You mean to destroy the alien ship, Captain?

...

Kirk: If the aliens go unpunished, they'll be back, attacking other Federation installations.

---

35 Rick Worland, "Captain Kirk: Cold Warrior," *Journal of Popular Film & Television* 16, no. 3 (1988): 110.
36 Mark P. Lagon, "'We Owe It to Them to Interfere:' *Star Trek* and U.S. Statecraft in the 1960s and the 1990s," in *Political Science Fiction*, eds. Donald M. Hassler, and Clyde Wilcox (Columbia: University of South Carolina Press, 1997), 235.
37 Keith M. Booker, "The Politics of Star Trek," in *The Essential Science Fiction Reader*, ed. J.P. Telotte (Lexington: University Press of Kentucky, 2008), 197.
38 While Nicholas Evan Sarantakes thoughtfully acknowledges that *Star Trek* cannot be reduced to pro-American propaganda, he, nevertheless, holds that "In episodes involving foreign policy, the Klingons represent the Soviet Union." Nicholas Evan Sarantakes, "Cold War Pop Culture and the Image of U.S. Foreign Policy: The Perspective of the Original *Star Trek* Series," *Journal of Cold War Studies* 7, no. 4, (2005): 78; also see Evanthis Hatzivassiliou, "Images of the International System and the Cold War in *Star Trek*, 1966–1991," *Journal of Cold War Studies* 23, no. 1 (2021): 55–88.

Spock: I merely suggested that a regard for sentient life.
Kirk: There's no time for that. It's a matter of policy. Out here, we're the only policemen around. And a crime has been committed. ·

Later, we learn that the matter is not as simple as Kirk believed. It turns out that the Federation colony was in Gorn space, and they viewed it as an invasion. Upon hearing the Gorn side of things, McCoy acknowledges that "we could be in the wrong" and "the Gorn simply might have been trying to protect themselves." In the end, Kirk decides to spare the life of the captain of the Gorn ship that destroyed the Federation colony.

Klingons are not a critique of the dark-skinned (as fatuously asserted by Bernardi) but of empire. The Klingon polity is the *Klingon Empire*. Star Trek posits the clearest critique of empire in all of American popular culture: "Mirror, Mirror" (1967). "Mirror, Mirror" opens with a discussion between Kirk and the leader of the "Halkans" (named "Tharn"). The Halkans refuse to allow the Federation to mine the dilithium crystals on their planet because "dilithium crystals represent awesome power. Wrongful use of that power, even to the extent of the taking of one life, would violate our history of total peace." Kirk asks "When may we resume discussion?" Tharn: "The council will meditate further, but do not be hopeful of any change." Tharn adds: "Captain, you do have the might to force the crystals from us, of course." Kirk: "But we won't."

Through a technical glitch, the Enterprise landing party is transported to an alternate universe. The Enterprise exists in this alternate universe, but instead of the Federation the political authority is the "Empire" – where "behavior and discipline" is "brutal, savage." While in the Federation universe the Enterprise only pursues peaceful means with the Halkans, in the Empire universe Kirk is "ordered to annihilate the Halkans unless they comply. *No alternative.*"

Conclusion

Star Trek (original series) is a historically important feminist and antiracist (Enlightenment) text. Star Trek of the 1960s was a major blow to the Jim Crow U.S. South – arguably the nail in its coffin. Millions of

Americans viewed a future totally free of ethnic biases – where African Americans (along with everyone else) are able to reach the highest echelons of society. While Star Trek was without question a metaphor for ethnic/gender justice and fairness, the original series also directly, unambiguously challenged the Jim Crow South – "Let that Be Your Last Battlefield". Additionally, the original series took on the proponents of anti-communism – many of which who sought to stigmatize and repress the civil right movement by denouncing it as part of a global communist cabal.

Star Trek of the 1960s has not received its due as a significant factor in the defeat of Jim Crow. There is little question that the original series exposed the lie and stupidity of ethnic bigotry. With such characters as Lt. Uhura, Abraham Lincoln, and Lokai, Star Trek played a glaring role in making the claims of the civil rights movement commonsensical – whereas (Southern) white supremacy and racial hatred were treated as fundamentally backward, as well as inherently malevolent and destructive.

Importantly, *Star Trek* openly identified the oppressive and destructive aspects of 1950s patriarchy. The pigeonholing of women into marriage; a disfiguring etiquette; the forcing of women to choose between marriage or career; as well as the debilitating discrimination against women who sought careers. *Star Trek* also portrayed the historic (ongoing) mistreatment of women – as currency; sex slaves; their killing to maintain family honor. *Star Trek* also led the way in the sexual revolution – as sex was a salient theme: highlighting female sexuality through provocative dress; women as sexually assertive; sex outside of marriage.

Star Trek featured strong, capable female characters. Characters that defiantly challenged patriarchy and were sharply politically cognizant. The creators of Star Trek were also sensitive to the perils of making sex and sexuality glaring – specifically pointing to the biases created by physical beauty. Finally, Star Trek pointed to the inter-generational friction created in part by the sexual (feminist) revolution of the 1960s.

Chapter Four

The Early Cold War and *Star Trek* (Original Series)

The Star Trek franchise (its broadcast iterations) is the quintessential text of modernity.[1] The franchise is also the prime text of contemporary modernism.[2] Here I outline how *Star Trek* (the original series) is the salient text of the Cold War. *Star Trek* brings into sharp relief the political controversies at the heart of the Cold War: anticommunism; economic modernization; the anti-colonial movement. The most acute point made in the Star Trek text of the 1960s on the Cold War is that anticommunism is a continuation of the German Nazi myopia to destroy the Soviet Union. More significantly, the episode "Patterns of Force" (1968) is an argument that the stoking of anticommunism created a political momentum\ milieu that Presidents Eisenhower (1953–1961) and Kennedy (1961–1963) failed to control. Put most philosophically, the politics of hate at the center of American anticommunism overwhelmed the voices of moderation and resulted in the American war in Vietnam (1965–1973).

1 George A. Gonzalez, *The Politics of Star Trek: Justice, War and the Future* (New York: Palgrave Macmillan, 2015).
2 George A. Gonzalez, *Justice and Popular Culture: Star Trek as Philosophical Text* (Lanham, MD: Lexington Books, 2019).

Anticommunism as Nazism

Anticommunism was a well-defined politics – namely, that communism was nothing more than an implacable cabal run out of the Kremlin and must be destroyed through continuous external pressure. The dogma of anticommunism has a clearly articulated, official manifesto: George Kennan's (1947) "The Sources of Soviet Behavior" (in *Foreign Affairs*). This document is broadly credited with outlining the U.S. policy of containment directed at the Soviet Union.[3] This, in fact, is not the case. Containment policy was actually specified by the Council on Foreign Relations (CFR).

Foreign policy planning in the U.S. for the post-World War II period was conducted by the CFR. During the war the State Department did not have the resources necessary to devote to policy-planning for the post-War period. So drawing on a grant from the Rockefeller Foundation,[4] the CFR became the primary organization planning for the time when the War would end, and in this planning effort it collaborated closely with the Department of State.

Since its inception in 1921 the CFR has been an economic elite-led policy discussion group designed to treat questions of foreign affairs.[5] During its early history the CFR received significant financial

3 John Lewis Gaddis, *Strategies of Containment: A Critical Appraisal of Postwar American National Security Policy* (New York: Oxford University Press, 1982), chap. 2.

4 Inderjeet Parmar, "'To Relate Knowledge and Action': The Impact of the Rockefeller Foundation on Foreign Policy Thinking During America's Rise to Globalism 1939–1945," *Minerva* 40, no. 3 (2002): 236–63.

5 Laurence H. Shoup, and William Minter, *Imperial Brain Trust: The Council on Foreign Relations and United States Foreign Policy* (New York: Monthly Review Press, 1977); G. William Domhoff, *The Power Elite and the State* (New York: Aldine de Gruyter, 1990), chap. 5, and *The Corporate Rich and the Power Elite in the Twentieth Century* (New York: Routledge, 2020), chap. 12.

Political scientist Clyde W. Barrow explains that "corporations emerged as the dominant economic institutions in capitalist societies by the end of the nineteenth century." He goes on to note that as early as the late 1920s "the bulk of U.S. economic activity, whether measured in terms of assets, profits, employment, investment, market shares, or research and development, was concentrated in the fifty largest financial institutions and five hundred largest nonfinancial corporations." Clyde W. Barrow, *Critical Theories of the State* (Madison: University of Wisconsin Press, 1993), 17. Also see Thomas Piketty, *Capital in the Twenty-First Century*, trans. Arthur Goldhammer (Cambridge, MA: Belknap Press, 2014); Patricia Cohen, "Study Finds Global Wealth Is Flowing to the Richest," *New York Times*, Jan. 19, 2015, B6; Gerry

contributions from Chase National Bank, Standard Oil of New Jersey, IBM, General Motors, General Electric, Texaco, and the National City Bank of New York.[6] Inderjeet Parmar, who has written extensively on the CFR,[7] describes in the following the corporate director positions held by the 55 CFR directors for the years 1921–1946:

> The fifty-five leaders held at least seventy-four corporate directorships ... The corporations concerned were among the largest in the United States: Myron C. Taylor of U.S. Steel and AT&T; Leon Fraser, Owen D. Young and Philip D. Reed of General Electric; Clarence M. Wooley and Lewis W. Douglas of General Motors; R.C. Leffingwell of J.P. Morgan and Co.; and Frank Polk, Douglas, John H. Finley, David F. Houston, and Reed of Mutual Life Insurance Company of New York.[8]

Reflective of the elite social standing of CFR directors during this period, the fifty-five directors of Parmar's study "held, on average, at least three

Mullany, "World's 8 Richest Have as Much Wealth as Bottom Half, Oxfam Says," *New York Times*, Jan. 16, 2017. Web.

   Political Scientists Jeffrey A. Winters and Benjamin I. Page, writing in 2009, hold that "it is now appropriate to ... think about the possibility of *extreme* political inequality, involving great political influence by a very small number of extremely wealthy individuals." They go on to add that "we argue that it is useful to think about the U.S. political system in terms of oligarchy." Jeffrey A. Winters, and Benjamin I. Page, "Oligarchy in the United States," *Perspectives on Politics*, Vol. 7, No. 4, 2009: 744, emphasis in original; also see Paul Krugman, "Oligarchy, American Style," *New York Times*, Nov. 4, 2011, A31, and "The Undeserving Rich," *New York Times*, Jan. 20, 2014, A17; Jeffrey A. Winters, *Oligarchy* (New York: Cambridge University Press, 2011); David Leonhardt, "All for the 1%, 1% for All," *New York Times*, May 4, 2014, MM23; Nicholas Kristof, "An Idiot's Guide to Inequality," *New York Times*, July 24, 2014, A27; Neil Irwin, "Economic Expansion for Everyone? Not Anymore," *New York Times*, Sept. 27, 2014, B1; Robert Frank, "Another Widening Gap: The Haves vs. the Have-Mores," *New York Times*, Nov. 16, 2014, BU4.

6   Laurence H. Shoup, "Shaping the National Interest: The Council on Foreign Relations, the Department of State, and the Origins of the Postwar World, 1939–1943," (Ph.D. Thesis, Northwestern University, 1974), 42.

7   Inderjeet Parmar, "The Issue of State Power: The Council on Foreign Relations as a Case Study," *Journal of American Studies* 29, no. 1 (1995): 73–95, " 'Mobilizing America for an Internationalist Foreign Policy': The Role of the Council on Foreign Relations," *Studies in American Political Development* 13 (fall 1999): 337–73, and *Think Tanks and Power in Foreign Policy: A Comparative Study of the Role and Influence of the Council on Foreign Relations and the Royal Institute of International Affairs, 1939–1945* (New York: Palgrave Macmillan, 2004).

8   Parmar, "The Issue of State Power", 82.

[elite social club] memberships, with the Cosmos and Metropolitan clubs in Washington, DC, and Century and Knickerbockers of New York, being the most popular. In all, 170 club memberships were reported."[9]

The involvement of the CFR in setting the trajectory for the U.S.'s post-War foreign policy has been thoroughly documented and discussed.[10] As Parmar notes, "From 1939 onwards, the Council, in collaboration with the State Department, established the War and Peace Studies Project, the aim of which was to outline the national interests of the USA as a basis for official planning for a post-war foreign policy."[11] Geographer Neil Smith observes that the CFR's War and Peace Studies project "established a vital foundation for State Department postwar planning."[12]

The key policy principle put forward by the CFR in its War and Peace Studies project was the "Grand Area" concept. The basic idea is that the U.S. needed a "Grand Area" of the globe "in order for its economy to function without fundamentally changing."[13] When put forward in 1942, this vital area was to comprise the "Western Hemisphere, Continental Europe and Mediterranean Basin (excluding Russia), the Pacific Area and the Far East, and the British Empire (excluding Canada)."[14] The CFR advised that "to integrate the Grand Area, the United States was to develop institutions for international financial

---

9 Ibid.
10 Harley Notter, *Postwar Foreign Policy Preparation, 1939–1945* (Washington, D.C.: U.S. Government Printing Office, 1949); Shoup, "Shaping the National Interest"; Shoup and Minter, *Imperial Brain Trust*; Robert D. Schulzinger, *The Wise Men of Foreign Affairs: The History of the Council on Foreign Relations* (New York: Columbia University Press, 1984); Domhoff, *The Power Elite and the State*, chap. 5; Parmar, "The Issue of State Power", "'Mobilizing America for an Internationalist Foreign Policy'", and "'To Relate Knowledge and Action'"; Neil Smith, *American Empire: Roosevelt's Geographer and the Prelude to Globalization* (Berkeley: University of California Press, 2003); Laurence H. Shoup, *Wall Street's Think Tank: The Council on Foreign Relations and the Empire of Neoliberal Geopolitics, 1976–2014* (New York: Monthly Review Press, 2019); David M. McCourt, *American Power and International Theory at the Council on Foreign Relations, 1953–54* (Ann Arbor: University of Michigan Press, 2020).
11 Parmar, "The Issue of State Power", 83.
12 Smith, *American Empire*, 331.
13 Parmar, "The Issue of State Power", 83.
14 Shoup, "Shaping the National Interest", 109.

collaboration; for international monetary exchange; to resolve raw materials problems; and so on."[15]

These policy prescriptions would in the main presage U.S. foreign policy throughout the Cold War. Most importantly, the Grand Area concept became embodied in U.S. containment policy. This policy sought to limit the Soviet bloc within its post-World War II area, with the expectation that by hemming in the Soviet Union and its satellites their long term economic and political viability would be undermined. While put forward as an assertive policy directed at the Soviet Union (albeit not a militarily confrontational one), U.S. containment policy sought to keep the global area viewed as necessary by the CFR for the functioning of the U.S. market economy within the Western allies' sphere of influence.[16] In this way containment policy allowed the West to regain and maintain its economic dynamism, while seeking to stifle that of the Soviet bloc.

Therefore, Kennan (a member of the CFR) in his essay did not outline containment strategy as broadly understood – with Kennan only using the term *containment* once in his disquisition. What Kennan does do is offer a political rationale for engaging the Soviet Union in a cold war – baldly asserting that Soviet leaders are inexorably impelled by their psychology, ideology, and history "to overthrow the political forces beyond their borders."[17] In this way Kennan is arguing that the U.S. should pick up where the Nazis left off – but instead of directly attacking the Soviet Union the U.S. should use its "power to increase enormously the strains under which Soviet policy must operate" and thereby "promote tendencies which must eventually find their outlet in . . . the break-up . . . of Soviet power."[18] Kennan strikes a Nazi-like stance when he vilifies dissenters from anti-communist dogma as traitors:

---

15 Parmar, "The Issue of State Power", 83.
16 Domhoff, *The Power Elite and the State*, chap. 5; George A. Gonzalez, *Urban Sprawl, Global Warming, and the Empire of Capital* (Albany: State University of New York Press, 2009), chap. 5.
17 George F. Kennan ("X"), "The Sources of Soviet Conduct," in *Essential Readings in World Politics*, eds. Karen A. Mingst, and Jack L. Snyder, 3rd ed. (New York: W.W. Norton, 2008), 29.
18 Ibid., 33.

By the same token, exhibitions of indecision, disunity and internal disinte-
gration within this country have an exhilarating effect on the whole communist movement. At each evidence of these tendencies, a thrill of hope and
excitement goes through the communist world; a new jauntiness can be noted
in the Moscow tread; new groups of foreign supporters climb on to what they
can only view as the band wagon of international politics; and Russian pressure increases all along the line in international affairs.[19]

Supportive of the idea of anticommunism as a continuation of German
Nazism is historian Paul Hanebrink's 2018 book, *A Specter Haunting
Europe: The Myth of Judeo-Bolshevism*. Hanebrink holds that a common
theme to both Nazism and post-war anticommunism was the false
notion that Jewish identity played an outsized role in the Soviet Union
and the communist movement.[20]

The position that anticommunism is a continuation of Nazi myopia
is supported by the fact that key architects of American foreign policy in the post-World War Two period were the Dulles brothers – John
Foster Dulles and Allen Dulles.[21] John Foster Dulles would serve as
Secretary of State for almost the entirety of the Eisenhower administration (only resigning upon imminent death in 1959), and Allen Dulles as
head of the CIA (Central Intelligence Agency) from 1953 until 1961. John
Foster's political stature is reflected in the fact that Washington Dulles
airport is named after him. It is noteworthy that the Dulles brothers
were prominent members of the CFR – with Allen serving as its president (1946–1950).[22]

John Foster was a senior partner of Sullivan and Cromwell – a
prominent Wall Street law firm.[23] As a leader of the firm he was keen
to cultivate a lucrative relationship with Corporate Germany.[24] John
Foster, if not pro-Nazi, was a public defender of the Hitler government

19 Ibid.
20 Paul Hanebrink, *A Specter Haunting Europe: The Myth of Judeo-Bolshevism* (Cambridge,
MA: Belknap Press, 2018).
21 Stephen Kinzer, *The Brothers: John Foster Dulles, Allen Dulles, and Their Secret World
War* (New York: Henry Holt, 2013).
22 Wikipedia: Members of the Council on Foreign Relations, accessed Nov. 13, 2019. Web.
23 Nancy Lisagor, and Frank Lipsius, *A Law Unto Itself: The Untold Story of the Law Firm
Sullivan & Cromwell* (New York: William Morrow, 1988).
24 Ibid., chap. 8.

in the 1930s – actively minimizing the threat the regime posed to world peace and to Jews.[25]

Allen Dulles, while a partner of Sullivan and Cromwell, became chief operative for the Office of Strategic Services (the precursor to the CIA) in Switzerland during the war. Allen prioritized maintaining his contacts among the Nazis leadership – including Himmler, while at the same time burying, minimizing reports of the Holocaust. Allen believed that the real threat was the Soviets.[26]

The idea that U.S. anticommunism is picking up the baton from the Nazis on the question of the Soviet Union can be read into the *Star Trek* episode "Patterns of Force". In "Patterns of Force" a renown Federation historian is sent to a relatively primitive planet (Ekos) as a "cultural observer." Nevertheless, in an effort to stabilize the planet's society the historian models its politics on Nazi Germany. With Nazism as the political basis of Ekos, the Ekosians organize around the vilification of Zeons – a population from the neighboring planet of Zeon. ("Why do the Nazis hate Zeons?" "Because without us to hate, there'd be nothing to hold them together. So the Party has built us into a threat, a disease to be wiped out.") John Foster Dulles understood that the Grand Area concept alone wouldn't mobilize the American public into action, and recognized that anticommunism (hate toward the Soviet Union) would seemingly do the job.[27] In the episode "Day of the Dove" (1968) an alien is surreptitiously fostering animosity between the Enterprise crew and Klingons on broad – Captain Kirk rhetorically asks: "Has a war been staged for us, complete with . . . ideology and patriotic drum beating?"

Where "Patterns of Force" breaks new ground is in the observation that anticommunism cannot be controlled, effectively managed. While both Presidents Eisenhower and Kennedy publicly embraced, promoted anticommunism, both sought stable relations with the Soviet Union. This effort to curb the excesses of anticommunism failed, which

25 Ibid., 132 and 140.
26 Neil H. Petersen, ed., *From Hitler's Doorstep: The Wartime Intelligence Reports of Allen Dulles, 1942–1945* (University Park: Pennsylvania State University Press, 1996), 12; David Talbot, *The Devil's Chessboard: Allen Dulles, the CIA, and the Rise of America's Secret Government* (New York: Harper, 2015), chaps. 1 and 2.
27 Gaddis, *Strategies of Containment*, 136.

resulted in the American war in Vietnam – where the U.S. military tallied success by the number of "enemy" dead (the same measure of success employed by the Nazis with regard to the Holocaust), and conducted the wanton bombing of North Vietnam that killed tens-of-thousands.[28] The Federation official (named Gill) that established the Ekos Nazi state (and who adopted the role of Führer in the regime): "felt that such a state, run benignly, could accomplish [Nazi] efficiency without sadism." Gill: "At first it worked," but he was sidelined (drugged into a stupor by subordinates) and a genocidal campaign was begun in earnest against the Zeons.

In the case of Eisenhower – contrary to Kennan's argument of placing maximum stress on the Soviet Union – he did not want an arms race with the Soviet Union.[29] Immense pressure was placed on his administration to ramp up spending on armaments[30] – one presidential aide derisively spoke of the "Democratic Agitation Cabal" for the party's glaring role in creating an atmosphere of alarm on the military threat from the Soviets.[31] It was seemingly this pressure that prompted Eisenhower to warn of a "Military-Industrial Complex" in his farewell address.[32]

Many understood Eisenhower's admonishment as directed particularly against military contractors – the so-called merchants of death,[33] and perhaps this is what Eisenhower thought was the source of the effort to usurp his authority as President. The idea of the political push for increased military spending coming specifically, predominantly from the defense industry is belied by the Gaither Committee. This committee was appointed by Eisenhower in 1957 after the Soviet's

---

28 Pierre Asselin, *Vietnam's American War: A History* (New York: Cambridge University Press, 2018).
29 Helen Bury, *Eisenhower and the Cold War Arms Race: "Open Skies" and the Military-Industrial Complex* (New York: I.B. Tauris, 2014).
30 Ira Chernus, *Apocalypse Management: Eisenhower and the Discourse of National Security* (Stanford: Stanford University Press, 2008).
31 As quoted in James Ledbetter, *Unwarrated Influence: Dwight D. Eisenhower and the Military-Industrial Complex* (New Haven: Yale University Press, 2011), 90.
32 Ledbetter, *Unwarrated Influence*.
33 James McCartney, and Molly Sinclair McCartney, *America's War Machine: Vested Interests, Endless Conflicts* (New York: Thomas Dunne Books, 2015).

launch of Sputnik – to issue policy assessments and recommendations on the state of defense preparedness and technology. The commission came forward with a conclusion that put it at odds with Eisenhower (but consonant with Kennan's anti-Soviet treatise) – advising a substantial increase in military spending.[34] The Gaither Committee was headed initially by an official from the RAND corporation – a leading think tank on military, foreign policy issues. The subsequent two directors did have ties to the defense industry. The Advisory Panel to the committee, however, drew from the broader corporate community – Brown Bros., Harriman (a leading investment firm); Shell Oil; Chase Manhattan Bank; the Ford Foundation; Bell Telephone Laboratories; the Columbia Broadcasting System (CBS).[35] This indicates that the Gaither Committee reflected broader corporate elite thinking, and not solely that of the defense industry.

Soviet-American Relations Under Eisenhower and Kennedy

In addition to keeping a lid on defense spending, Eisenhower sought to stabilize relations with the Soviet Union through leadership summits. Eisenhower's openness to meeting with Soviet leaders to ease tensions and arrive at mutual understandings to attain relaxed, even peaceful relations ran contrary to Kennan's anti-Kremlin stance. Kennan held that the Soviet Union in its international relations was fundamentally, inveterately untrustworthy. Any agreements with the Soviets were motived by subterfuge aimed to gain a long-term tactical, strategic advantage. Put differently, the Soviet Union had no interest in peace, except insofar that peace aided it in its sinister machinations. Again, Kennan is unabashed in his contempt, hostility toward the Soviet government: "It must invariably be assumed in Moscow that the aims of

---

34 David L. Sneed, *The Gaither Committee, Eisenhower, and the Cold War* (Columbus: Ohio State University Press, 1999).

35 Security Resources Panel of Science Advisory Committee (a.k.a. the Gaither Committee), Deterrence and Survival in the Nuclear Age (Washington, DC: Executive Office of the President, 1957 Nov. 7), 31.

the capitalist world are antagonistic to the Soviet regime and, therefore, to the interests of the peoples it controls. *If the Soviet Government occasionally sets its signature to documents which would indicate the contrary, this is to be regarded as a tactical maneuver in dealing with the enemy.*"[36] Given this stance, peace agreements with the Soviets are not only futile but treasonous, as such agreements are presumed to be materially aiding Soviet aggressiveness. This is how the idea of "mutual co-existence" came to be viewed by anticommunists as an effort to weaken the U.S. and strengthen the Soviet Union.[37]

There is reason to think that anticommunists began to think of Kennedy, in particular, as a traitor to the cause. This reasoning is seemingly reflected in a November 1, 1963, memo produced by American military intelligence. In reporting on Cuban exiles training in Fort Benning (Georgia) it was noted that exiles have concluded that the Kennedy government is pursuing a "principle of co-existence" toward the Castro regime and expressing this argument to their military superiors.[38] Kennedy in his famous June 1963 American University commencement address directly rejected Kennan's reasoning on treaty-making with the Soviet Union. He declared that "even the most hostile nations can be relied upon to accept and keep those treaty obligations, and only those treaty obligations, which are in their own interests"[39] – openly indicating that the Soviets can be trusted to keep their word on agreements which both sides uphold. Kennedy, while saliently speechifying on the dangers of communism, would perhaps equally as conspicuously make public statements indicating opportunities for the establishment of global peace and harmony. One historian notes that "the tendency to portray international communism as an implacable and efficient monolith while at the same time acknowledging its

---

36 Kennan, "The Sources of Soviet Conduct", 31, emphasis added.
37 Michael Lindsay, *Is Peaceful Co-Existence Possible?* (East Lansing: Michigan State University, 1960).
38 INSCOM/ISF (U.S. military intelligence), "Memo: Summary of Information," Nov. 1, 1963, Record # 194-10013-10448, p. 267.
39 U.S. President John F. Kennedy, "Commencement Speech: American University, June 10, 1963," in *"Let the Word Go Forth": The Speeches, Statements, and Writings of John F. Kennedy*, ed. Theodore C. Sorensen (New York: Delacorte Press, 1988), 286.

frailties and vulnerabilities – grow more noticeable under Kennedy."[40] In "Patterns of Force" Gill (after rescued by the Enterprise crew) was shot/killed while giving a televised speech renouncing the genocidal policies enacted by his underlings. The same fate as Kennedy's.[41]

Eisenhower-Kennedy on the *Developing World*

Where Kennedy and Eisenhower parted ways on foreign policy was in regard to the developing world. Eisenhower was inclined to suppress so-called Third World nationalism when it was perceived to threaten American interests. This is most clearly evident with the 1953 operation to overthrow a democratically-elected nationalist government in Iran (operation Ajax) and install the pro-Western, dictatorial Shah,[42] as well as with the U.S. backed overthrow in 1954 of a democratically-elected government in Guatemala that was a threat to Corporate America's property holdings in that country.[43]

Kennedy was more apt to engage the anti-colonial (nationalist) movement and seek to steer it toward American-style democracy. Kennedy was attracted to W.W. Rostow's *The Stages of Economic Growth: A Non-Communist Manifesto* and made Rostow an official in his government.[44] As suggested by the title of the book, Rostow put forward an argument that societies, including developing ones, could achieve an ideal level of political/economic development through a process of market-guided, non-revolutionary, evolution. Following from this Kennedy sought to encourage the advancement or "modernization" of

---

40 Gaddis, *Strategies of Containment*, 206.
41 George A. Gonzalez, *Popular Culture, Conspiracy Theory, and the Star Trek Text* (Lanham, MD: Lexington Books, 2020), chap. 4.
42 Mike de Seve, *Operation Ajax: The Story of the CIA Coup that Remade the Middle East* (New York: Verso, 2015).
43 Piero Gleijeses, *Shattered Hope: The Guatemalan Revolution and the United States, 1944-1954* (Princeton: Princeton University Press, 1992).
44 Kimber Charles Pearce, *Rostow, Kennedy, and the Rhetoric of Foreign Aid* (East Lansing: Michigan State University Press, 2001).

developing countries through foreign aid and by promoting political/ policy reforms, as well as technology sharing.[45]

Two *Star Trek* original series episodes stand out for their criticism of American client states in the *developing world*: "Piece of the Action" (1968) and "The Cloud Minders" (1969). These episodes indicate that such states are hopelessly corrupt, and overtly opposed to reforms that could threaten their power.

"A Piece of the Action" involves a remote planet (Sigma Iotia II) a Federation ship visited a 100 years ago. This contact distorted the planet's society because the ship left behind a book dealing with "Gangsters. Chicago. Mobs. Published in 1992." "They seized upon that one book as the blueprint for an entire society. As the Bible." As a result the society of Sigma Iotia II organized itself into a set of competing mafia organizations – where the mobs themselves are the government. This is similar to the distortion that occurred in *underdeveloped* countries when they were incorporated into the American world system. In many *underdeveloped* societies rentier/compradore classes came to dominate, as they offer raw materials and cheap labor to multi-national corporations. Such countries are characterized by corruption and authoritarian practices.[46] The following exchange in "A Piece of the Action" occurs between women on the street and a mafia lieutenant:

> **Women:** When's the boss going to do something about the crummy street lights around here, eh? A girl ain't safe. And how about the laundry pickup? We ain't had a truck by in three weeks.
>
> **Mafia Henchman:** Write him a letter.

---

45 Michael E. Latham, *Modernization as Ideology: American Social Science and "Nation Building" in the Kennedy Era* (University of North Carolina Press, 2000); Nils Gilman, *Mandarins of the Future: Modernization Theory in Cold War America* (Baltimore: Johns Hopkins University Press, 2007).

46 Jacqueline S. Ismael, *Kuwait: Dependency and Class in a Rentier State* (Gainesville: University of Florida Press, 1993); Giovanni Arrighi, with Beverly Silver, *Chaos and Governance in the Modern World System* (Minneapolis: University of Minnesota Press, 1999); Immanuel Wallerstein, *World-Systems Analysis: An Introduction* (Durham: Duke University Press, 2004); Harold Kerbo, *World Poverty: The Roots of Global Inequality and the Modern World System* (New York: McGraw-Hill, 2005).

Women: He sent it back with postage due. We pay our percentages.
We're entitled to a little service for our money.
Henchman: Get lost, will ya? Some people got nothing to do but complain.

Prioritizing stability and expediency, the Enterprise crew sets on the following course: "Oxmyx is the worst gangster of all [on this planet]. We quarrel with Oxmyx' methods, but his goal is essentially the correct one. This society must become united or it will degenerate into total anarchy." Just as the New York mafia did with Costa Nostra in the 1930s,[47] the Enterprise establishes a federated political structure employing the planet's mafia groups: "You people, you've been running this planet like a piecework factory. From now on, it's going to be under one roof. You're going to run it like a business. *That means you're going to make a profit."*

"Cloud Minders" is centered on Adrana – a planet divided into a rigid caste system. The Stratos dwellers live a life of opulence, high art, and contemplation in a cloud city. Troglytes live on the barren surface slaving away in mines – with little to show for their arduous labor. When the government of Adrana is told of technology that could allow for the full equality of Troglytes, it rejects this technology arguing that such a proposal "could only cause more unrest among" the Troglytes. Adrana's leader complains that (because of Kirk's efforts at reform) he "knows nothing except how to destroy our power."

Conclusion

Star Trek of the 1960s draws us into the similarities between Nazism and anticommunism. What is particularly striking about "Patterns of Force" is the seeming argument that the hate, animosity of anticommunism could not be controlled in the ways that both Presidents Eisenhower and Kennedy sought to do so. By the time that this Star Trek episode aired the American military was unleashed in what can be considered a wanton military campaign in Indo-China. What politically fueled

---

47 Selwyn Raab, *Five Families: The Rise, Decline, and Resurgence of America's Most Powerful Mafia Empires* (New York: St. Martin's Griffin, 2006); Letizia Paoli, *Mafia Brotherhoods: Organized Crime, Italian Style* (New York: Oxford University Press, 2008).

this wanton killing was the hate of unvarnished, unmediated anti-communism – in a similar fashion that the Holocaust was fueled by unhinged, raging Nazi hate. Arguably, the American state turned to a complete reliance on military force, violence in Indo-China because its client state in South Vietnam was impervious to progressive reforms. This is ostensibly the assertion put forward in "The Cloud Minders"[48] and "Piece of the Action".

---

48 Taking an optimist turn, Captain Kirk is able to fashion a progressive outcome to the plot of the episode.

Chapter Five

Star Trek and the *Clash of Civilizations*: Anti-Enlightenment versus Modernism (Universal Justice)

Samuel P. Huntington in his "Clash of Civilizations" concept holds much of the world is rooted in "traditionalism." As such, Huntington rejects the Enlightenment – as he argues that traditionalist societies (mostly *underdeveloped* countries) are resistant to modernity (secularism, democracy, gender equality, etc.). In contradistinction to modernity, traditionalists advocate state imposed religion (i.e., theocracy); paternalism (i.e., male dominance); obscurantism. Significantly, much of the broadcast Star Trek franchise illustrates Huntington's conceptualization of world politics – particularly beginning with *The Next Generation* series.

Most importantly is Huntington's argument that world politics is centered on "civilizations" – each with their own distinct culture and politics. Star Trek depicts this *clash of civilizations* politics; gives insight into it; and allows us to see what is at stake. The world of Star Trek is populated by a number of "civilizations" – most prominently the Federation civilization; the Klingon civilization; the Romulans; and the Cardassians. The Federation civilization reflects the modernism of

the Western world; the Klingons, Romulans, and Cardassians are traditionalist societies.

Universal Civilization versus Traditionalism

Huntington points to the concept of "universal civilization": "The idea
implies in general the cultural coming together of humanity and the
increasing acceptance of common values, beliefs, orientations, practices, and institutions by peoples throughout the world."[1] Huntington
holds the notion of a *universal civilization* is misplaced, and instead
holds that people are irrevocably wedded to their idiosyncratic group
characteristics: "People define themselves in terms of ancestry, religion,
language, history, values, customs, and institutions. They identify with
cultural groups: tribes, ethnic groups, religious communities, nations."
Huntington describes "politics", in large part, as an effort of "people .
. . to define their identity." Moreover, "nation states remain the prin-
cipal actors in world affairs . . . [and] their behavior is shaped . . . by
cultural preferences, commonalities, and differences." Therefore, concepts of universal civilization are unworkable because "humanity is
divided into subgroups – tribes, nations, and, at the broadest level, civilizations."[2] Ultimately, Huntington holds that most civilizations hold to
traditionalism, and the West's conceptualization of a universal civilization (i.e., the values of modernity) are in actuality only the values of the
West. Moreover, the West needs to protect itself, and its values, from the
threat of traditionalist civilizations.

Prior to the *Enterprise* (2001–2005) series, Star Trek rejects
Huntington's view of universal civilization, and openly argues that
humanity must embrace such a notion if it is to establish a thriving
society. The concept of universal civilization advocated by Star Trek is
rooted in Marxist ideas of political change and Marxist social/economic

---

1 Samuel P. Huntington, *The Clash of Civilizations and the Remaking of World Order*
   (New York: Simon & Schuster, 1996), 56; also see David Brooks, "Saving the System,"
   New York Times, April 29, 2014, A23; Ross Douthat, "Vladimir Putin's Clash of
   Civilizations," *New York Times*, Feb. 27, 2022, SR9; Ezra Klein, "The Enemies of
   Liberalism Are Showing Us What It Truly Means," *New York Times*, April 4, 2022, A19.
2 Huntington, *The Clash of Civilizations*, 21.

ideas. This suggests that when Huntington holds that the idea of *universal civilization* is in essence a fiction, he is in fact objecting to Marxism.

Federation, Modernity, and Marxism

The *federation* concept of polity in Star Trek is ostensibly predicated on the Marxist ontology of social change and revolution. Karl Marx argued that a classless society based on modernity would occur through a series of progressive revolutions. Leon Trotsky, as leader of the Russian Revolution (1917), held that this revolution would inspire other societies to have their own socialist revolution, and, thus, the revolutionary polity would be expanded globally through such examples as set by Russia (and presumably) *et al.*[3]

Viewing Star Trek through the prism of American Trotskyism, the franchise can be read as offering a *telos* that results in a socialist revolution. As outlined in Chapter Two, (reflecting Trotskist reasoning/hope in terms of U.S. history)[4] to the Revolutionary War ("Omega Glory" 1968 – original series), the Civil War ("Savage Curtain" 1969 – original series), Star Trek adds to America's revolutionary "moments" with the "Bell Uprising" – a critique/rejection of *neoliberal* economics/politics. (Notably, in the *Deep Space Nine* episode that depicts this uprising – "Past Tense" [1995] – the term "Neo-Trotskyists" is used.) Star Trek is not only critical of the economics and politics of *neoliberalism*, but it also takes aim at capitalism, as reflected in *The Next Generation* episode "The Neutral Zone" (1988) (see Chapter One). In *Star Trek: Discovery* (2017-present) "capitalism" is expressly linked to slavery and predatory foreign policy machinations ("There Is a Tide..." 2021). In Chapter One I additionally explain that according to Star Trek humans by the 24th century have undergone a profound paradigm shift in values and outlook

---

3   Issac Deutscher, *The Prophet Armed: Trotsky 1879–1921*, vol. 1 (New York: Oxford University Press, 1963); Leon Trotsky, *History of the Russian Revolution* (New York: Pathfinder, 1980 [1933]).

4   Bryan D. Palmer, *James P. Cannon and the Emergence of Trotskyism in the United States, 1928-38* (Boston: Brill, 2022).

– as depicted in the *Deep Space Nine* episode "Little Green Men" (1995). The point is made that humanity's (America's) values have shifted away from "currency-based economics" and toward a "philosophy of self-enhancement" (*Deep Space Nine* – "In the Cards" 1997).

With humanity basing itself on a "philosophy of self-enhancement", humans come to lead the Federation, and, most importantly, its expansion is predicated on voluntary merger/union. ("The Federation is made up of over a hundred planets *who have allied themselves* for mutual scientific, cultural and defensive benefits" [*Deep Space Nine* – "Battle Lines" 1993]. "The Federation consists of over one hundred and fifty different worlds *who have agreed to share their knowledge and resources in peaceful cooperation*" [*Voyager* – "Innocence" 1996].) Captain Kirk, speaking of the founders of the Federation: "They were humanitarians and statesmen, and they had a dream. A dream that became a reality and spread throughout the stars, a dream that made Mister Spock and me brothers."

Indicative of seemingly how the social justice politics (broadly conceived – i.e., *universalism*) of the Federation transcends all ethnic, religious (species) divisions, Spock, when asked "do you consider Captain Kirk and yourself brothers?", replied: "Captain Kirk speaks somewhat figuratively and with undue emotion. However, what he says is logical and I do, in fact, agree with it" ("Whom Gods Destroy" 1969 – original series). Captain Picard declares: "If there's one ideal the Federation holds most dear it's that all men, all [alien] races, can be united" (*Star Trek: Nemesis* 2002). During a *Next Generation* 1990 episode, a visiting alien is very impressed with the highly diverse background of the Enterprise crew: "Truly remarkable . . . These people ... they're all so different from one another ... yet they work together freely." ("Transfigurations" 1992).

Voyager episode "The Void" (2001) provides insight into the normative values and political processes that are at the center of *federation*. Voyager is trapped in a "void" in space (where there is no "matter of any kind"). Other ships trapped in the void have taken up the practice of attacking/raiding other trapped ships for supplies as a means of surviving. ("There are more than one hundred fifty ships within scanning range but I'm only detecting life signs on twenty-nine of them.")

Through collaboration and solidarity, Captain Janeway argues the ships in the Void can work together to escape. In shaping this reasoning, Janeway draws inspiration from the example of the Federation: "The Federation is based on mutual co-operation. The idea that the whole is greater than the sum of its parts. Voyager can't survive here alone, but if we form a temporary alliance with other ships maybe we can pool our resources and escape." Voyager shares its limited food and medical supplies, as well as joins in common defense, to build trust and establish (what Janeway calls) the "Alliance." Through the Alliance, Voyager's food supplies are enhanced: "One of the crews that joined us had technology that tripled our replicator efficiency. . . we can feed five hundred people a day now using half the power it took us a few days ago." Led by Voyager, the Alliance ships escape the Void. Those that refused to become members stay behind.

Therefore, Star Trek posits the argument that a stable, ethical society can only be based on a classless society based on modernism – one that is free of gender and ethnic biases. Nonetheless, the creators of the franchise offer a somewhat sympathetic treatment of a traditionalist society via the Klingons.

Traditionalism in Star Trek: The Klingons

Unlike the Federation, which is based on the universal ideas of equality; fairness; and equal treatment, Klingons are traditionalists. Traditionalist societies tend to be patriarchies, as is Klingon society – with women prohibited from sitting on the Klingon's supreme political body, the "High Council"; political decisions for the family/clan are made by the eldest male; and the crimes of fathers implicate their sons ("Sins of the Father" 1990, "Reunion" 1990 and "Redemption" 1991 – all *Next Generation* episodes).

The fictional Klingons base their polity on ethnic identity – hence, the name of their polity, the *Klingon* Empire. (Klingons in fact are not a different species from humans, as Klingon-human couplings can result in offspring.)[5] Klingons look to their past and religion to shape

5   This is also true of Vulcans-humans and Romulans-humans.

and legitimatize their politics. The episode "Rightful Heir" (1993 – *Next Generation*) focuses on the figure of Kahless, who is credited with founding the Klingon state. According to Klingon theology, Kahless "united" the Klingons; gave them "honor and strength"; and "promised to return one day and lead us again." Kahless is described as a prophet-like figure in the following: "To believe in Kahless and his teachings ... and to become truly Klingon." Kahless is cloned from ancient DNA material, and the Kahless clone is made head of the state for the Klingon Empire.

Daniel Bernardi in *Star Trek and History: Race-ing toward a White Future* holds that *The Next Generation* conveys a bias against dark-skinned people.[6] He writes the "biological notion of blackness is displaced onto the Klingons while a civilized notion of whiteness is ascribed to the Federation."[7] Bernardi correctly notes that Klingons (which are brown-skinned) are described as inherently violent. In "The Icarus Factor" (1989) the point is explicitly made by the steadfastly objective Data that "there is, of course, a genetic predisposition toward hostility among all Klingons."

Bernardi, in my estimation, is wrong to argue that the Klingons represent dark-skinned people *writ large*. Instead, the Klingons represent traditional societies (*à la* Huntington). The Romulans in *The Next Generation* are cast as implacable and dangerous foes. (Significantly, Romulans are not generally dark-skinned.) They are described as "violent beyond description"; also "their belief in their own superiority is beyond arrogance" ("The Neutral Zone").

Another polity rooted in ethnic identity (i.e., traditionalism) is the Cardassian Alliance. In "Chain of Command" (1992 – *Next Generation*) the Cardassians are discovered to be marshaling their forces along the Federation border and readying for an invasion. The invasion is only stopped because the Enterprise is able to attach explosives to the Cardassian attack fleet – the Cardassians agree to forego their planned assault in exchange for the disarming of the explosives attached to their ships.

---

6   Daniel Leonard Bernardi, *Star Trek and History: Race-ing toward a White Future* (New Brunswick, NJ: Rutgers University Press, 1998), chap. 4.
7   Ibid., 133.

While traditionalist societies in Star Trek are cast as violent and dangerous, they are also cast as the technological equal of the Federation – the quintessential modernist society. This leads to two important conclusions. First, that according to Star Trek, in terms of technology, modernist societies are not superior to traditionalist ones. This is an explicit rejection of the Enlightenment claim that technological advancement occurs most freely where social progress (political equality and equal treatment) is predominant.[8] Second, that traditional societies (i.e., the *underdeveloped world*) are not dependent and subordinate to modernist (i.e., Western) societies. Both these conclusions support Huntington's claim that traditionist societies can out-maneuver modernist societies, and that the modernist/traditionalist bifurcation is the prime tension in the contemporary world system. Put differently, that colonialism; resource and labor exploitation; and Western military (political) interventions are peripheral to the fact that *developing world* politics and economics are essentially autonomous, and can overrun the West.

Modernity as a Form of Traditionalism

Huntington's most controversial assertion is that the West should abandon the notion that modernism (the Enlightenment) is truly universal, and accept the conclusion that modernity is a type of traditionalism. More precisely, that Western concepts of political equality, secularism, and equal treatment are exactly that – *Western!* More ominously, unless we in the West give up the misguided idea that democracy (in all its dimensions) is a universal principle, the West may succumb to competing civilizations – those rooted in conventional notions of traditionalism. Huntington holds that: "The survival of the West depends on Americans reaffirming their Western identity and Westerns accepting their civilization *as unique not universal* and uniting to renew and preserve it against challengers from non-Western societies." Worse still, the West has to accept the patriarchy; authoritarianism; and

---

8   Robert C. Scharff, and Val Dusek, eds., *Philosophy of Technology: The Technological Condition*, 2nd ed. (New York: Wiley-Blackwell, 2014).

political religiosity of traditional societies – i.e., not seek to change them. Huntington, somewhat pessimistically, asserts that "avoidance of a global war of civilizations depends on world leaders accepting and cooperating to maintain the multicivilizational character of global politics."[9]

What Star Trek shows is that a world dominated by this outlook, where there is no universalism but only parochialism and sectarianism, is a world dominated by instability; war; authoritarianism; and racism. This thinking is particularly portrayed with the Klingons (below). The Cardassians have a military dictatorship. They invaded the neighboring planet of Bajor and occupied it for decades – enslaving its population and exploiting its natural resources. Similarly, the Romulan government maintains a regime of terror as "thousands of dissidents . . . live in fear of their lives" (Next Generation – "Face of the Enemy" 1993).

The political instability/corruption of Klingon politics and the uncertainty of the Federation/Klingon alliance is evident in the Next Generation episodes "Sins of the Father"; "Reunion"; "The Mind's Eye" (1991); and "Redemption". In "The Mind's Eye" a Klingon colonial governor (Vagh) suspects that the Federation is arming an independence movement in the colony (Krios) he governors. The brutality of the Klingons is conveyed when a Klingon ambassador (Kell) is asked: "You are prepared to grant [the inhabitants of Krios] independence?" Kell responds: "Perhaps. But we will conquer them again later if we wish to." At one point, war between the Federation and the Klingon Empire almost occurs when the Enterprise is seemingly caught red-handed delivering weapons to the rebels. (The weapons were transported from the Enterprise by Chief Engineer Geordi Laforge, who, under the control of the Romulans, was actively seeking to de-stabilize Klingon-Federation relations.) The Enterprise is surrounded by a number of Klingon battleships and ordered to stay in planetary orbit. It is reported that Governor Vagh "is fully prepared to fire upon the Enterprise."

In "Sins of the Father" Worf's father is posthumously found to have betrayed the Klingons to the Romulans (a rival nation-state) – resulting

9   Huntington, The Clash of Civilizations, 21, emphasis added.

in the destruction of a Klingon spacestation. Worf (who is Klingon and an Enterprise officer) challenges this verdict – risking execution in doing so. It turns out that the allegation against Worf's father was fabricated to maintain the stability of Klingon politics (as it was the patriarch of a currently powerful family/clan that was the actual traitor). Worf's "challenge was defeated before he ever made it. ... If the truth were known, it would ... almost certainly plunge [the Klingon Empire] into civil war." When Captain Picard refuses to accept the outcome of a corrupt judicial/political process that would result in his officer's execution, the Klingon chancellor (K'mpec) warns him "if you defy the orders of the High Council in an affair of the empire, the alliance with the Federation could fall to dust."

In "Reunion" we learn that "the Klingon Empire is at a critical juncture." It "may be facing civil war." It is further observed that "Klingon wars seldom remain confined to the Empire ... the Federation won't be able to stay out of it for long." The action is precipitated by the fact that the Klingon chancellor is dying. (He was slowly poisoned.) The internal Klingon political situation is so uncertain that Captain Picard (a non-Klingon) is asked to serve as "arbiter of succession" – thereby overseeing the process whereby a successor chancellor will emerge. In "Redemption" civil war among the Klingons does subsequently erupt. One of the two factions vying for political power is led by the Duras family: "The Duras family is corrupt and hungry for power. . . . They represent a grave threat to the security of the Federation." (The Federation, under the leadership of Captain Picard, exposes the military relationship between the Duras clan and the Romulans, thereby allowing the pro-Federation Gowron-led faction to win the Klingon civil war.) In "Reunion", during the succession deliberations, a Duras foot solider carries out a suicide attack (with a bomb placed inside his arm) in an effort to disrupt the proceedings.

Perhaps the worst aspect of a world permanently cleaved into *civilizations* is the xenophobia and racism that would seemingly be forever part of global politics – both in the *developed* (or *advanced*) world and the rest. The xenophobia of traditionalism (e.g., the Klingons) is evident when Worf is chided for bringing "*outsiders* [i.e., humans] to our Great Hall" ("Sins of the Father"). In another instance, one Klingon is opposed to another Klingon marrying a non-Klingon: "She believes that by bringing aliens into our families we risk losing our identity as Klingons." This is acknowledged as "a prejudiced, xenophobic view" (*Deep Space Nine* – "You Are Cordially Invited" 1997).

The racism inherent in the *civilization* concept posited by Huntington is particularly evident in *The Next Generation* episode "Birthright" (1993). The action centers on a prison camp established by the Romulans over 20 years earlier to house a group of Klingons who could not return home. They were stigmatized by the fact that they were taken prisoner – Klingons are expected to fight to the death or commit suicide if captured. As an act of kindness, and at great sacrifice, a Romulan officer agrees to oversee the camp – otherwise the captured Klingons would be executed. Worf – whose father was falsely rumored to be at the camp – discovers it. He objects to an arrangement whereby Klingons live as prisoners of the Romulans – even though they are treated well; have complete freedom on the planet they reside on; have given birth to children; and share a strong sense of community. Worf, nevertheless, tells the Romulan camp commander (Tokath) that "you robbed the Klingons of who they were. *You dishonored them.*" Tokath, pointing to the irrationality of Worf's position, retorts: "By not slitting their throats when we found them unconscious?" Worf explicitly resorts to racialist thinking to justify his position: "I do not expect you to understand. *You are a Romulan.*" Hence, there is something *particular* about Klingons, and it is inscrutable to non-Klingons. Tokath explains "we've put aside the old hatreds. Here, Romulans and Klingons live in peace." Worf is unmoved: "Do not deceive yourself. These people are not happy here. I see the sadness in their eyes."

Worf adopts an openly hateful attitude when he comes to discover that a woman (Ba'el) he is romantically interested in is an offspring of one of the Klingon prisoners and a Romulan. Worf is kissing Ba'el, draws back her hair and sees her pointed ears (characteristic of Romulans). Outraged Worf exclaims "*You are Romulan!*" Unabashed in his hate, he asks with a tone of disgust: "*How could your mother mate with a Romulan?*" He declares "*it is an obscenity!*" Fully venting his racism, Worf tells Ba'el: "Romulans are *treacherous, deceitful*. They are without honor." Ba'el: "My father is a good man. He is kind, and generous. There is nothing dishonorable about him."

Earth-Vulcan Relations in *Enterprise*

The most demoralizing aspect of Huntington's clash of civilizations claim is the view that the West is unique in its commitment to (or suitability for) modernism or the Enlightenment (democracy, equality, fairness), which would invariably lead to a type of hostility in the West toward societies that are at least perceived to be doomed to traditionalism (as argued by Huntington). Most notably, Huntington holds (as outlined above) the West is in competition with the rest of the world (dominated by traditionalism). This reasoning is at the core of the Star Trek television series, *Enterprise*. Perhaps the most salient aspect of the *Enterprise* narrative is that unlike in the original series where the Vulcans and Earthlings are part of the same Federation polity/civilization, in this series Earth and Vulcan have an uneasy relationship and seemingly form two discrete (competing) civilizations.

It is significant that in the movie *Star Trek: First Contact* (1996) by 2063 San Francisco is destroyed.[10] In the episode "Past Tense" (*Deep Space Nine*) San Francisco is where the *anti-neoliberalism* Bell Uprising occurs in 2024 (i.e., the basis of a new global politics). Thus, according to *First Contact* Earth's global polity is not formed as a result of the replacement of the *neoliberal* order. Instead, Earth's politics is predicated on a WE/THEY distinction – as it is "first contact" with the Vulcans that prompts humanity to mobilize into forming global government. ("It unites humanity in a way no one ever thought possible when they realize they're not alone in the universe.")   This is consonant with Huntington's point that "for peoples seeking identity and reinventing ethnicity, *enemies are essential.*"[11]

---

10 Referring to San Francisco: "Beautiful city. Used to be, anyway. I didn't think anyone still lived there." From an initial script of the movie: https://www.scriptslug.com/assets/scripts/star-trek-first-contact-1996.pdf
11 Huntington, *The Clash of Civilizations*, 20, emphasis added.

Therefore, the political foundation of humanity in the mid-21st century is the WE/THEY dichotomy – with the Vulcans serving as "They" – and this is the basis of *Enterprise* (set in the 22nd century, whereas the original series and *Discovery* are set in the 23rd century and *Next Generation; Deep Space Nine; Voyager* in the 24th). In *Enterprise* conflict/competition with the Vulcans does occur. "The Forge" (2004), "Awakening" (2004), and the "Kir'Shara" (2004) is a three episode story arc whereby Earth's embassy on Vulcan is bombed, killing Admiral Forrest (Captain Archer's mentor), and the Enterprise crew gets swept up in internal Vulcan religious and political strife – with an effort made against Captain Archer's life; and the Enterprise and Vulcan military ships coming to a face-off. In the denouement we learn that elements within the Vulcan government were behind the bombing of the Earth embassy, and that a faction still in the government wants to pull the planet toward a political/military alliance with the Romulans. An intention ominously threatening to Earth as it suggests the formation of a Vulcan-Romulan civilization (they are the same ethnicity).

Especially telling for a politics based on competing *civilizations*, *Enterprise* conveys Earth's polity as afflicted with xenophobia and racism. The series concludes in 2005 and the penultimate episode centers on the group "Terra Prime" (episode title). Initially, this organization is described as xenophobic: "They want to stop all contact with alien species." "They believe it's corrupting our way of life." Later, we learn that Terra Prime is racist: "This is an alien-human hybrid. Living proof of what will happen if we allow ourselves to be submerged in an interstellar coalition. Our genetic heritage. . ." "That child is a cross-breed freak. How many generations before our genome is so diluted that the word human is nothing more than a footnote in some medical text?" The leader of Terra Prime declares, "I'm returning Earth to its rightful owners." Referring to signs of broad sympathy for Terra Prime and its agenda, the Vulcan Ambassador Soval notes: "The fact that [Terra Prime] has the support of so many of your people is . . . troubling."

Of great significance for a discussion based on Huntington's vision of world politics informed by the idea of conflictive *civilizations* is the Xindi – introduced in *Enterprise*. The Xindi are the former inhabitants of the planet Xindi. The Xindi are cleaved into five distinct *civilizations*, with each civilization corresponding to a distinct species: one insectoid; one humanoid; aquatic; ape-like; and reptilian. As a result of their competition, the Xindi destroyed their planet: "The war went on for nearly a hundred years. . . . The insectoids and reptilians detonated massive explosions beneath the eight largest seismic fissures. I'd like to think they didn't realize how devastating the result would be."[12] During the onset in 2022 of the great power (the U.S., NATO, Russia) conflict over Ukraine,[13] public officials (and experts) openly spoke of engaging nuclear weapons – which could result in the destruction of the human race.[14]

Conclusion

Star Trek, beginning with the original series, conveys the positive/inclusive politics predicated on the universalism of modernity (i.e., the Enlightenment). This politics, and the process that brings them about, is ostensibly shaped by the social justice politics inherent in Marxism, and, more specifically, Trotskist thinking. Beginning with *The Next Generation* series, Star Trek begins drawing on ideas and arguments consonant with the *clash of civilizations* (the anti-Enlightenment) ideation posited by Samuel P. Huntington. Particularly significant is the Klingons – which represent a traditionalist society. Other traditionalist societies conveyed in Star Trek (i.e., those centered on ethnic identity) are the Romulans and the Cardassians. These traditionalist polities are perennially hostile and militarily aggressive toward each other and

---

12 (*Enterprise* – "The Shipment" 2003).
13 David E. Sanger, and Steven Erlanger, "Fear That War Will Spill Over Borders," *New York Times*, April 28, 2022, A1.
14 Max Fisher, "Thoughts Turn to the Unthinkable: A Spiral Into a Nuclear War," *New York Times*, March 17, 2022, A12; William J. Broad, "Smaller Bombs Raise a Specter Of Atomic War," *New York Times*, March 22, 2022, A1; David E. Sanger, Eric Schmitt, Helene Cooper, and Julian E. Barnes, "U.S. Makes Contingency Plans Lest Russia Use Its Most Potent Weapons," *New York Times*, March 24, 2022, A10; William J. Broad, "Orbital Fleet Warily Eyes Russia's Atomic Arsenal," *New York Times*, April 6, 2022, A9; David E. Sanger, and Julian E. Barnes, "Putin May Be Tempted to Use Small Nuclear Weapon, C.I.A. Chief Says," *New York Times*, April 15, 2022, A8.

the modernist Federation (i.e., the *clash of civilizations* as envisioned by Huntington).

In illustrating the *clash of civilizations* concept, Star Trek shows that to accept this *clash* as the permanent basis of global politics is to consign humanity to perpetual authoritarianism; instability; and war. Perhaps most disconcerting is that cleaving the globe into distinct civilizations results in irreparable racialist reasoning and ethnic-based animus ("Birthright"). *Enterprise* depicts how operating on the assumption of competing *civilizations* leads to xenophobia, racism, and hate even in the West ("Terra Prime"). Ultimately, the *clash of civilizations* risks planetary destruction (the Xindi).

The analytical brilliance of Star Trek is found in its creators' ability to effectively and credibly convey both Marxist politics and values, and the *clash of civilizations* ideation, as well as to entertainingly and convincingly juxtapose these competing worldviews. As a result, Star Trek makes an outstanding and invaluable contribution to political theory and international relations theory. Most significantly, it demonstrates the hope and optimism evident in Marxism and the demoralization and pessimism that inheres in Huntington's anti-Enlightenment *clash of civilizations* view of humanity and global politics.

Chapter Six

Nazi Takeover of America: *The Man in the High Castle* and Star Trek

The Trump government was predicated on virulent nationalism (including nods to white supremacy)[1] and Trump himself tried to orchestrate the overturning of the 2020 election (in part) through the Jan. 6th (2021) storming of the U.S. Capitol.[2] If Trump had succeeded in maintaining himself in the U.S. presidency through extra-constitutional means (skullduggery), the result would have almost certainly been the end of American democracy and the imposition of dictatorship. *Amazon Prime* recently released *The Man in the High Castle* (2015-2019). The premise of the series is that it is 1962 in a United States that was conquered by the Nazis and Japanese as a result of World War Two. Significantly, this is

---

1 Kathleen Belew, "Militant Whiteness in the Age of Trump," in *The Presidency of Donald J. Trump: A First Historical Assessment*, ed. Julian E. Zelizer (Princeton: Princeton University Press, 2022).

2 Peter Baker, "Portrait of a Power Grab by a Would-Be Autocrat," *New York Times*, June 10, 2022, A1; Paul Krugman, "Crazies, Cowards and the Trump Coup," *New York Times*, July 1, 2022, A22; Peter Baker, "Trump Intent Out in Open," *New York Times*, July 4, 2022, A1; Danny Hakim, "Georgia Inquiry Is Subpoenaing 7 Trump Allies," *New York Times*, July 6, 2022, A1; Luke Broadwater, "Jan. 6 Panel Will Tie Trump To Extremists," *New York Times*, July 6, 2022, A10.

not the first portrayal in post-9/11 popular culture of a Nazi takeover of the U.S. The *Star Trek: Enterprise* episode "Stormfront" (2004) conveys a fictional reality where the Nazis control much of the Northeast United States, including New York City and Washington, DC.

The fictionalization of Nazi (and Imperial Japan) dictatorship controlling the U.S. suggests that at least significant segments of the public perceived the American polity moving significantly toward dictatorship prior to the events of Jan. 6 (2021). The fictional portrayal of American Nazi dictatorship points to three key factors: (1) viewers perceive the fact that Nazism has been imposed on the U.S.; (2) it suggests that the sacrifice the U.S. made in fighting World War Two as well as the Cold War was for naught; and (3) *the state within state* arrangement (whereby government authority is invested in secret, non-accountable elements) is inherently an authoritarian, dangerous political arrangement.

A Nazi Takeover of America's Government

Particularly in the aftermath of the U.S. invasion of Iraq, pundits, commentators began alleging that a coterie of right-wing extremists (broadly known as neoconservatives)[3] had hijacked (overtaken) the executive branch. The specific allegation was that a group of unelected policy elites with an aggressive, belligerent global agenda have come to control the American foreign policy apparatus.[4]

In 2002 as the neoconservative agenda (i.e., invading Iraq) was gaining momentum both through the Bush government and the national media – most prominently the *New York Times*[5] – the *Enterprise* episode "Fallen Hero" aired. The Enterprise picks up the Vulcan Ambassador to the planet of Mazar – she has been recalled by the her government.

---

3   Justin Vaïsse, *Neoconservatism: The Biography of a Movement* (Cambridge, MA: Harvard University Press, 2010).
4   Paul Krugman, "Nonsense And Sensibility," *New York Times*, August 11, 2006, A15; Craig Unger, *The Fall of the House of Bush: The Untold Story of How a Band of True Believers Seized the Executive Branch, Started the Iraq War, and Still Imperils America's Future* (New York: Scribner, 2007).
5   Don Van Natta, Jr., Adam Liptak, and Clifford J. Levy, "The Miller Case: A Notebook, A Cause, a Jail Cell and a Deal," *New York Times*, Oct. 16, 2005, sec. 1, p. 1.

Soon after Enterprise departs, the Mazar government demands that the Vulcan Ambassador (V'lar) return – sending ships in pursuit. After initially refusing to tell Enterprise Captain Jonathan Archer the cause of the current controversy, V'lar relents and informs the Captain why the Mazarites are so eager for her return:

> The Mazarites pursuing us are criminals. They are members of an organization that's infiltrated all levels of government, making themselves wealthy and powerful at the expense of many innocent victims. Their methods include eliminating anyone who stands in their way.

She adds that "the corruption ran deeper than I thought." *The Man in the High Castle* makes direct reference to the American invasion/conquest of Iraq when a Nazi bounty hunter invokes a *most wanted* deck of cards – a gimmick used by the American military during the 2003 conquest of Iraq.[6] He murders someone on one of these cards and publicly displays the body – allowing birds to feed on the corpse ("The Illustrated Woman" 2015).

Whether or not "Fallen Hero" is an apt metaphor for the politics that resulted in the U.S. invasion of Iraq (and there is strong evidence that it is[7]), the series *The Man in the High Castle* and the *Enterprise* episode "Stormfront" appear to tap into the reality that at least significant segments of the U.S. populous do not support the military adventurism of the Bush/Obama era, and the feeling that these policies are more so imposed on the public and less so a product of genuine public sentiment. The most significant manifestation of the American public's unsupportive attitude toward U.S. military policies abroad is the public's strong opposition to a military draft.[8] From the perspective of those that oppose such policies as the invasion of Iraq, and the torture tactics (discussed below) associated with such policies, the American

---

6 Editorial Board, "Justice for Iraq," *New York Times*, April 25, 2003, A30.
7 George A. Gonzalez, *Energy and the Politics of the North Atlantic* (Albany: State University Press of New York, 2013), chap. 6.
8 Darren K. Carlson, "Public Support for Military Draft Low," Gallup, Nov. 18, 2003. Web; "Military draft? Polls finds Americans Opposed," Associated Press, June 24, 2005. Web; Amy J. Rutenberg, *Rough Draft: Cold War Military Manpower Policy and the Origins of Vietnam-Era Draft Resistance* (Ithaca: Cornell University Press, 2019).

government is behaving like a modern-day Nazi, or imperial Japanese, regime. "Stormfront" and *The Man in the High Castle* fictionalize this reasoning.

The 2004 *Enterprise* episode "Stormfront" sends Captain Archer back to the World War Two period. History has been altered. Time traveling aliens are aiding the Nazis. The Nazis control much of the Northeast U.S., including New York City and Washington, D.C. Nazis occupy and operate from the White House: "We are inside the home of a former American President. It seems to me your war effort is going well enough." In *The Man in the High Castle* the Germans and Japanese have divided the U.S. – with the Nazis controlling that half east of the Rocky Mountains (renamed the Greater Reich) and the Japanese that part west of these mountains (designated the Japanese Pacific States) (the Rocky Mountains are a "neutral zone" and lawless). The Nazis in both "Stormfront" and *High Castle* engage in torture. This parallels U.S. torture policies beginning with the invasion of Afghanistan.

The Bush Administration in 2001 declares the "War on Terror", and as part of this war orders the invasion of Afghanistan – where Al-Qaeda is headquartered. As the U.S. is taking prisoners in Afghanistan the Bush Administration designates many of them to be "enemy combatants" – therefore denying them Geneva Convention protections, including the prohibition against torturing prisoners of war.[9] The U.S. opens the Guantanamo prison camp in 2002 to house these so-called enemy combatants – where "aggressive interrogation" (i.e., torture techniques) against these prisoners were authorized.[10] The movie *Zero Dark Thirty* (2012) (made in close collaboration with the U.S. military and the Central Intelligence Agency) indicates that torture is used by the U.S. government in its dealings abroad.[11] Additionally, in 2013 the *New York Times* reported that "A nonpartisan, independent review of interrogation and

9 Editorial Board, "Rewriting the Geneva Conventions," *New York Times*, August 14, 2006, A20.

10 Richard W. Stevenson, "White House says Prisoner Policy Set Humane Tone," *New York Times*, June 23, 2004, A1.

11 Scott Shane, "Portrayal of C.I.A. Torture in Bin Laden Film Reopens a Debate," *New York Times*, Dec. 13, 2012, A1; Editorial Board, "About Those Black Sites," *New York Times*, Feb. 18, 2013, A16.

detention programs in the years after the Sept. 11, 2001, terrorist attacks concludes that 'it is indisputable that the United States engaged in the practice of torture' and that the nation's highest officials bore ultimate responsibility for it."[12]

The episode *Enterprise* "Anomaly" aired September 2003 and offers a storyline whereby torture is needed to protect Earth from attack. This paralleled Bush Administration arguments at the time that "enhanced interrogation" techniques were required to protect the U.S. from further attack.[13] Shortly after entering the Delphic Expanse to stop the planned destruction of Earth, the Enterprise's fuel stock is pirated: "They took every one of our antimatter storage pods." Without these pods, Enterprise will run out of fuel in a month – "tops". In the raid against Enterprise one of the pirates is captured. Information from this captive (Orgoth) is the only way that Enterprise can retrieve its much needed fuel. Archer tries to intimidate Orgoth into cooperating, but Orgoth holds that "I don't think you'd be very comfortable torturing another man. You and your crewmates are far too civilized for that. Too moral." Captain Archer tells him otherwise: "I need what was stolen from me. There's too much at stake to let my morality get in the way." Orgoth: "Are you taking me to your torture chamber?" Archer puts Orgoth in an "airlock" – which Archer uses to suffocate Orgoth. Orgoth relents and tells the Captain what he wants to know. Enterprise recovers her much needed fuel. The use of suffocation as a torture technique in *Enterprise* is significant in that the most prominent torture technique deployed by the Bush Administration was "waterboarding" – whereby victims feel as if they are suffocating through simulated drowning.[14]

---

12 Scott Shane, "U.S. Practiced Torture After 9/11, Nonpartisan Review Concludes," *New York Times*, April 16, 2013, A1; also see Mark Mazzetti, "Panel Faults C.I.A. Over Brutality Toward Terrorism Suspects," *New York Times*, Dec. 10, 2014, A1; Carol Rosenberg, "War Crimes Hearing Revisits Abuses Meted by U.S. Troops," *New York Times*, May 2, 2022, A8, and "Psychologist Describes Fearing for Prisoner at C.I.A. Black Site," *New York Times*, May 4, 2022, A22; Carol Rosenberg, and Julian E. Barnes, "Witness Says Haspel, Before Becoming C.I.A. Chief, Observed Use of Waterboard," *New York Times*, June 4, 2022, A17.

13 "Effort to Prohibit Waterboarding Fails in House," Associated Press. March 12, 2008. Web.

14 Scott Shane, "Waterboarding Used 266 Times on 2 Suspects," *New York Times*, April 20, 2009, A1.

The Man in the High Castle casts torture as a tool used to intimidate and punish political opponents. Torture is standard Nazi, Imperial
Japanese policy, used against those who run afoul of either regime.
Political opponents are referred to as "Semites" – a racial slur. The
viewer is shown instances of people tortured for purposes of maintaining order. To fully understand the use of torture, the idea of *intersubjective agreement* must be taken into account.

American philosopher, Richard Rorty, writing in the early 1980s, in
fashioning *neopragmatism* argues that societies are based on *intersubjective agreement.*[15] Thus, what is required for societal stability is enough
consensus on a set of ideas – any set of ideas. Hence, what matters is
consensus, and not the ideas themselves. Presumably, when there is
not enough intersubjective consensus/agreement, then social/political
breakdown occurs.

Over 10 years before Rorty published his path-breaking notion of
intersubjective agreement the *Star Trek* episode "Mirror, Mirror" (1967)
aired. This original series episode, outlined in Chapter Three, aptly pres-
ages Rorty's reasoning. Humans lead a vast interstellar organization in
both the Empire and Federation universes – each with a radically different politics. "Mirror, Mirror" depicts the idea, as Rorty would later
argue, that the content of society's political values do not matter – what
matters is the consensus (*intersubjective agreement*) achieved around
those values. With the *neopragmatism* conceptualization of society as
little more than *intersubjective agreement*, the prime goal of institutions is
achieving societal cohesion by fashioning, fostering, and/or imposing
such agreement. Therefore, authoritarian (dictatorial) regimes, as well
as torture practices/technologies, can be effective (even appropriate)
means to maintain (impose) *intersubjective agreement* – thereby establishing political/social stability.

One important conclusion from Star Trek's treatment of the *intersubjective agreement* argument is those societies that prioritize achieving

---

15 Richard Rorty, *Philosophy and the Mirror of Nature* (Princeton: Princeton University
Press, 1981); Michael Bacon, *Richard Rorty: Pragmatism and Political Liberalism*
(Lanham, MD: Lexington Books, 2007); Neil Gross, *Richard Rorty: The Making of an
American Philosopher* (Chicago: University of Chicago Press, 2008).

such agreement, as opposed to those that base their cohesion on the attainment of justice, democracy, etc., develop/deploy technologies intended to impose political consensus – or, at least, to suppress/punish those that would challenge this consensus. In the Empire (of "Mirror, Mirror" and later "In a Mirror, Darkly" [2005 – *Enterprise*]) torture technologies called an "agoniser" and an "agony chamber" exist. The agony chamber is also depicted in *Star Trek: Discovery*, when the Discovery visits the Empire universe ("Vaulting Ambition" and "What's Past Is Prologue" – both 2018). When used they cause extreme pain without causing tissue damage. "In a Mirror, Darkly" the following is explained of the "agony booth": "Traditional forms of punishment can overwhelm the nervous system. After a time, the brain ceases to feel anything." "These sensors continually shift the stimulation from one nerve cluster to another, keeping the subject in a constant state of agony." Thus, pain can endlessly be inflicted. Such fictional technologies presage the 2003 Bush Administration notorious memo authorizing torture. In this memo perpetual, intense pain was deemed legally allowable. Only "death, organ failure or permanent damage resulting in a loss of significant body functions will likely result" were prohibited.[16] While the Bush Administration didn't develop infinite pain machines (i.e., agonisers or agony chambers) (as far as we know), technologies/practices like "water boarding" (where drowning is simulated) were used hundreds of times on individual victims.[17]

It is through such means that the Empire (in "Mirror, Mirror") maintains stability – most importantly, threatens/menaces those that seek to operate outside of (or challenge) its *intersubjective agreement* regime. Communicating the political theory at the heart of the Empire: Spock explains that "Terror must be maintained or the Empire is doomed. It is the logic of history." As noted above, the original series episode "Cloud Minders" (1969) depicts a society (the planet of Ardana) where torture technology ("the rays") is used to maintain/stabilize a caste system.

---

16 As quoted in Mark Mazzetti, "'03 U.S. Memo Approved Harsh Interrogations," *New York Times*, April 2, 2008. Web.
17 Shane, "Waterboarding Used 266 Times on 2 Suspects"; Jonathan Hafetz, "Don't Execute Those We Tortured," *New York Times*, Sept. 25, 2014, A31; Mazzetti, "Panel Faults C.I.A. Over Brutality Toward Terrorism Suspects."

The use of the threat of torture (and worse) to politically cow a populace is dramatically depicted in the *Next Generation* episode "Face of the Enemy" (1993). Enterprise's ship counselor, Deanna Troi, is impressed into impersonating an officer from the Romulan secret police – known as the "Tal Shiar." Troi is forced into a mission whereby as this officer (named "Major Rakal") she is to oversee the transport of special cargo to the Federation. As a Tal Shiar officer, Troi is able to order a Romulan ship captain into transporting this secret shipment – high ranking members of the Romulan government who wish to defect. They are in boxes – suspended in "stasis."

Troi, at first, is disoriented and frightened – as she was drugged; kidnaped; surgically altered (without her knowledge); and literally thrust into the role of a Tal Shiar officer abroad an enemy military ship. (If Troi were to be found out she "will be killed.") Troi, however, has empathic abilities (i.e., able to sense the emotions of others), and she quickly realizes that the Romulans on the ship are petrified of her – a Tal Shiar officer. ("They're all terrified of me.") Her Romulan collaborator explains to Troi: "The purpose of the Tal Shiar is to ensure loyalty [i.e., subservience to the Romulan *intersubjective agreement*]. To defy them is to invite imprisonment ... or death." We learn that the Romulan government maintains a regime of terror to maintain political stability as "thousands of dissidents [i.e., those who challenge their society's *intersubjective agreement*] ... live in fear of their lives." When Major Rakal (Troi) decides to take command of the ship she threatens the bridge crew and their families: "If any one of you defies the Tal Shiar, you will not bear the punishment alone. Your families ... all of them, will be there beside you." They dutifully accede to her orders.

The Nazis/Japanese do not solely rely on torture to maintain stability in *The Man in the High Castle*. They also use propaganda. Viewers are shown a political advertisement encouraging residents of occupied America to be *pragmatic*. They should focus on the fact that they have jobs and that they are contributing to a "strong" (i.e., stable) nation.

Star Trek, in the original series episode "Bread and Circuses" (1968), is ostensibly critical of *pragmatism* and its overriding emphasis on societal stability – with the outcome being the persistence of slavery worldwide. Harvard academic Louis Menand points out that the core of *pragmatism* is "the belief that ideas [ethics, morality] should never become ideologies" – which early pragmatists saw as the cause of the American Civil War.[18] Therefore, pragmatists seemingly hold that concepts of justice or political principles should not precede the goal of maintaining social stability. To do so invites devastating conflict (e.g., the American Civil War) and chaos. The Enterprise crew, in "Bread and Circuses", comes upon a planet that is virtually identical to mid-20th Earth (America); except on this world the Roman Empire never collapsed and, instead, spans the entire planet. "A world ruled by emperors who can trace their line back 2,000 years to their own Julius and Augustus Caesars." The result is that slavery continues – in part because the slave system was reformed to maintain its stability: "Long ago, there were [slave] rebellions" but "with each century, the slaves acquired more rights under the law. They received rights to medicine, the right to government payments in their old age, and they slowly learned to be content." Spock: "Slavery evolving into an institution with guaranteed medical payments, old-age pensions." In defending this society, one of the characters explains: "This is an ordered world. . . . There's been no war here for over 400 years." "Could your land of that same era make that same boast?", he asks of the Enterprise landing party (specifically Kirk and McCoy). Explaining why Federation citizens who had come upon this Rome-like world could not be allowed to leave (thereby having the opportunity to tell others of its existence): "I think you can see why they don't want to have their *stability* contaminated by dangerous ideas of other ways and places" – i.e., *ideologies* of freedom, democracy, equality, etc., that could be politically destabilizing. Spock, in response, opines: "given a conservative empire, quite understandable."

With the U.S. ostensibly operating as a traditional, conservative empire, a seeming pessimism has set in. This pessimism is manifest in the series *The Man in the High Castle*.

---

18 Louis Menand, *The Metaphysical Club* (New York: Farrar, Straus, and Giroux, 2001), xii.

The Politics of Pessimism

The Man in the High Castle and "Stormfront" both convey a pessimism on the current state of world affairs. This suggests that the optimism ("the end of history") of the victories over Nazism and Stalinist Russia has been lost. In the 1987 pilot episode of *Star Trek: The Next Generation* ("Encounter at Farpoint") the argument is explicitly made that the barbarism in human history is over. The all-powerful entity "Q" wearing a 1950s era U.S. military uniform: "You must return to your world and put an end to the commies. All it takes is a few good men." Captain Picard: "That nonsense is centuries behind us." Later in the episode, before a court convened by Q, Captain Picard proclaims: "We agree there is evidence to support the court's contention that humans have been murderous and dangerous. I say 'have been.'" In the 1987 episode "Lonely Among Us" Picard again suggests that the Cold War was "nonsense" (well in the past): "Do you understand the basis of all that *nonsense* between them?" Riker: "No sir. I didn't understand that kind of hostility even when I studied Earth history." Picard: "Oh? Well, yes, but these life forms feel such passionate hatred over differences in . . . strangely enough, economic systems." Thus, with the end of the Cold War humanity can expect a future of peaceful co-existence and humaneness.

The Man in the High Castle makes a number of references to American lives lost fighting the Nazis and the Japanese. One of the main characters (Juliana) had her father killed in the Pacific theater. A member of the resistance discusses in graphic terms how his comrades were killed fighting the Nazis. With the complete defeat of the U.S., these sacrifices are in vain. *The Man in the High Castle* is more pessimistic than "Stormfront" – as the *Enterprise* episode indicates in the denouement that the Americans are organizing a counter-offensive that will expel the Nazis from North America. Thus, Stormfront is more in the way of warning, whereas *The Man in the High Castle* suggests that World War Two, etc. were fought for no purpose, as wars of territorial conquest, torture, authoritarianism are the norm today, as they were during the

Nazi period. *The Man in the High Castle* describes how upon a Nazi takeover of America Jews in mass were killed.[19]

Authoritarianism

With a total Nazi/Japanese victory in *The Man in the High Castle*, authoritarianism is firmly entrenched. Today, authoritarianism is manifest as "the state within the state" (a.k.a. the "deep state") phenomenon. The U.S. foreign policy apparatus is the most insulated aspect of government – operating under a veil of secrecy (and misinformation [e.g., Iraq's WMDs]).[20] Former President Donald J. Trump recently complained that the U.S. *deep state* (within the American intelligence agencies/military) actively undermined his presidency.[21] *Star Trek: Deep Space Nine* in the 1990s specifically posited that *a state within the state* is a common practice throughout the world system. For the Federation, the state within the state is *Section 31*.

Section 31

Deep Space Nine introduces "Section 31" – a secret intelligence agency that is outside the law. It is described in the following terms: "We don't submit reports or ask for approval for specific operations, if that's what you mean. We're an autonomous department." In another instance, *Section 31* is cast as "judge, jury and executioner." *Section 31* justifies its existence and means in terms consonant with national security: "We deal with threats to the Federation that jeopardize its very survival."

19 Alexander Laban Hinton, *It Can Happen Here: White Power and the Rising Threat of Genocide in the US* (New York: New York University Press, 2021); Isabel Kershner, "Eichmann Talks and Talks In Nazi Tapes Riveting Israel," *New York Times*, July 5, 2022, A6.
20 Terry H. Anderson, *Bush's Wars* (New York: Oxford University Press, 2011); John Prados, *The Family Jewels: The CIA, Secrecy, and Presidential Power* (Austin: University of Texas Press, 2013); Mazzetti, "Panel Faults C.I.A. Over Brutality Toward Terrorism Suspects"; Michael P. Colaresi, *Democracy Declassified: The Secrecy Dilemma in National Security* (New York: Oxford University Press, 2014).
21 Julie Hirschfeld Davis, " 'Deep State'? Until Now, It Was a Foreign Concept," *New York Times*, March 7, 2017, A19.

"If you knew how many lives we've saved, I think you'd agree that the ends do justify the means."[22]

Section 31 operatives have no scruples. Prior to the advent of open hostilities between the Dominion and the Federation it infects the Changeling Odo (Chief of Security for Deep Space Nine) with a deadly disease in the hopes that he will infect the other Changelings (i.e., the Founders – the leadership caste of the Dominion).[23] (While Odo is a Changeling like the Founders, he rejects the Dominion and allies himself with the Federation.) Section 31 kidnaps a Starfleet officer (Julian Bashir – Chief Medical officer of Deep Space Nine); tortures him (through sleep deprivation); and psychologically disorients him into believing he is a Dominion spy. When Bashir states in disbelief: "Is it possible that the Federation would condone this kind of activity?" A Deep Space Nine crew member cynically responds: "I find it hard to believe that they wouldn't. Every other great power has a unit like Section Thirty-One"[24] – an all powerful, lawless secret security organization. The 2013 Star Trek movie, Into Darkness, has Section 31 conduct a false-flag operation to initiate war with the Klingons.

We learn that the Cardassians also operate a secret, autonomous intelligence service – the Obsidian Order. "In theory" the Obsidian Order "answer[s] to the political authority . . ., just as the military does. In practice we both run our own affairs."[25] Later, it is discovered that the Cardassian Obsidan Order and the Romulan Tal Shiar (another intelligence agency) secretly constructed a fleet of military ships, and unilaterally undertake an attack on the Dominion home world. ("If you attack the Dominion . . . . You'll be taking Romulus and Cardassia into war.")[26]

22 (Deep Space Nine – "Inquisition" 1998).
23 (Deep Space Nine – "Extreme Measures" 1999).
24 (Deep Space Nine – "Inquisition" 1998).
25 (Deep Space Nine – "Defiant" 1994).
26 (Deep Space Nine – "Improbable Cause" 1995).

Authoritarianism as a Threat to Human Civilization

Arguably, the most extreme and dangerous/destructive example of militarism/authoritarianism in human history is that of the German Nazi regime. Star Trek warns that Nazism and fascism pose profound threats for humanity and civilization. As noted above, in the original series episode "City on the Edge of Forever" (1967) the assertion is made that a Nazi victory in World War Two would have meant the ultimate end of civilization.

In *Star Trek: Voyager* "The Killing Game" (1998) a German Nazi officer emphasizes the putative greatness of Germany's past to justify its push for worldwide conquest:

> He's never embraced the Fuhrer or his vision. One does not co-operate with decadent forms of life, one hunts them down and eliminates them. The Kommandant speaks of civilization. The ancient Romans were civilised. The Jews are civilised. But in all its moral decay, Rome fell to the spears of our ancestors as the Jews are falling now. Look at our destiny! The field of red, the purity of German blood. The blazing white circle of the sun that sanctified that blood. No one can deny us, no power on Earth or beyond. Not the Christian Savior, not the God of the Jews. We are driven by the very force that gives life to the universe itself!

The kind of hyper-nationalism advocated by the likes of the Nazis is extremely dangerous in the modern era. Therefore, the parable of the Xindi (discussed above) and the fact that they destroyed their own planet must be taken seriously.

Much of the intrigue in *The Man in the High Castle* during season 1 revolves around the fact that the Germans have the atomic bomb, while the Japanese do not. This creates ambitions among certain of the Nazi political elite to engage in a war with Japan. A high ranking Nazi decides to pass along atomic weaponry science to the Japanese in the hopes of maintaining a balance of power, thereby avoiding another war. The Japanese high command expresses no desire for a balance of power, but seeks nuclear superiority in order to militarily overtake the Nazis.

With the politics of the state within the state, assassination becomes an effective political tool. Thus, authoritarianism means that political murder is a fact of political life.

The Politics of Assassination[27]

Star Trek makes the empirical claim that certain technologies exist in Empire that do not exist in Federation. As noted above, in the Empire exists an agony booth. Notably, when the Captain Archer of the Federation feels compelled to torture someone (to save planet Earth) he is forced to use conventional technology (an "airlock") to do so – in the process Archer comes close to killing the person (i.e., the torture victim) that has vital information (*Enterprise* – "Anomaly").

The *intersubjective agreement* argument in "Mirror, Mirror" is brought into sharper relief in *Deep Space Nine*, where the alternate universe is revisited a century later ("Crossover" 1994). We learn that Kirk's time in the alternate universe had a profound impact. "On my side, Kirk is one of the most famous names in our history." In "Mirror, Mirror" Kirk apprized Spock of a weapon ("the Tantalus field"). From one's quarters a person could zero in on victims and with the push of a button make them disappear. Kirk counseled Spock to use such technology to profoundly change the Empire, and base it on the values of the Federation. The end result is that the Empire collapses and Earth is occupied.

Focusing on the "Tantalus field", this is explicitly a technology of the Empire – as it does not exist in the Federation universe. The Tantalus field communicates key aspects of the structure and practice of political power in the context of *empire* (i.e., a polity whose priority is the maintenance of *intersubjective agreement*). (For *federation*, the priority is presumably justice – fairness, equality, transparency, etc.) Importantly, the concept of *intersubjective agreement* does not directly speak to the question of how many people, nor precisely who, has to participate in an *agreement* in order for society to be stable. Authoritarian polities (*empires*) seek to concentrate political and institutional authority in a

27 Benjamin F. Jones, and Benjamin A. Olken, "Do Assassins Really Change History?" *New York Times*, April 12, 2015, SR12.

small number of people – who exercise institutional control and work together to impose their *intersubjective agreement* on the whole of society.

In turn, this is precisely why the phenomenon of *palatial politics* occurs – people maneuver among the coterie of power wielders to hold and/or attain power. In the *Deep Space Nine* episode "When it Rains . . ." (1999) the argument is made that the Klingon Empire's current head of government (Chancellor Gowron) has no significant accomplishments other than successfully mastering Klingon "palace intrigue"[28]: "what has he done except plot and scheme his way to power."

In a context where political power is highly concentrated assassination becomes an effective means of advancing a military/political career (agenda) – as rivals/obstacles are vanquished. A plot is afoot during season 1 of *High Castle* to assassinate Hitler because he stands in the way of war against Japan. Allegations that Russian President Vladimir Putin aided in the installation of Donald J. Trump as U.S. President[29] can be interpreted as the effort to politically destroy Trump (i.e., character assassination) and replace his regime with one more hostile to Russia.[30] The Jan. 6th (2021) storming of the U.S. Capitol building was ostensibly an effort to block the installation of Joe Biden as U.S. President and maintain Donald Trump in office. At the core of this plot was the goal of appointing pro-Trump individuals to the College of Electors – the clutch of individuals that actually select the President.[31] In the Empire universe of "Mirror, Mirror" "Captain Kirk's enemies have a habit of disappearing" (via the Tantalus field). Spock (to Captain

---

28 In the *Star Trek: Voyager* episode "Author, Author" (2001) Klingon politics are referred to as "palace intrigue".
29 Matt Flegenheimer, and Scott Shane, "Bipartisan Voices Back U.S. Agencies on Russia Hacking," *New York Times*, Jan. 6, 2017, A1; Nicholas Fandos, and Sharon LaFraniere, "Two Reports on Meddling: Choose Your Own Verdict," *New York Times*, April 28, 2018, A14.
30 Editorial Board, "Mr. Trump and Mr. Putin, Best Frenemies," *New York Times*, June 29, 2018, A26; Michelle Goldberg, "Trump Shows The World He's Putin's Lackey," *New York Times*, July 17, 2018, A21; Sheryl Gay Stolberg, Nicholas Fandos, and Thomas Kaplan, "Measured Condemnation But No G.O.P. Plan to Act," *New York Times*, July 17, 2018, A1.
31 Jedediah Britton-Purdy, "We're Not a Real Democracy. That's Why Jan. 6 Happened," *New York Times*, Jan. 6, 2022, A23; Luke Broadwater, "Jan. 6 Panel Will Turn Over Evidence on Fake Electors to the Justice Dept.," *New York Times*, July 14, 2022, A15.

Kirk): "I do not intend to simply disappear as so many of your opponents have in the past." As alluded to above, Spock of the Empire uses the Tantalus field to gain the leadership of the Empire, and to fashion a new *intersubjective agreement*. The Klingon Empire's Chancellor, K'mpec, is poisoned to open the path to power for an ambitious clan (*Next Generation* – "Reunion" 1990). In the *Deep Space Nine* episode "Inter Arma Enim Silent Leges" (1999), a clandestine operation is successfully executed to manipulate the politics of the Romulan Empire by politically destroying a "Senator" to ensure the appointment of a reliable Federation ally to the Romulan "Continuing Committee" – the highest policymaking body in the Empire. Assassination resulting in the protection/entrenchment of a policy regime brings to mind the President John F. Kennedy assassination, as his killing seemingly cleared the way for a more reliable "Cold War Warrior" in Lyndon B. Johnson to ascend to the American presidency.[32]

Conclusion

The Man in the High Castle casts a politics where Nazism/fascism is the dominant global ideology, including the U.S. A similar scenario is portrayed in the *Star Trek: Enterprise* episode "Stormfront". Both *Star Trek: Enterprise* and *High Castle* give voice to critics who argue that U.S. post-9/11 military and torture policies have been imposed. With militarism and torture becoming the norm in global politics, Star Trek and *High Castle* indicate a demoralization of the current epoch and a broader pessimism – negating the optimism derived from the end of the Cold War and the defeat of Nazism/fascism in World War Two.

This demoralization/pessimism can account for the Trump phenomenon (virulent nationalism) and the effort to overturn the 2020 U.S. presidential election. Put differently, Trumpism is a product of the fact that American *democracy* is already failing. *High Castle* and Star Trek of the 1990s and 2000s dramatically portray the authoritarianism that characterize U.S. politics. This politics is executed through the

32 George A. Gonzalez, *Popular Culture, Conspiracy, and the Star Trek Text* (Lanham, MD: Lexington Books, 2020), chap. 4.

state within the state phenomenon – where the national security state is beyond democratic politics. In both *High Castle* and Star Trek such politics are depicted as inherently dangerous and threatening the very survival of the planet in the modern era (i.e., portend military competition leading to global nuclear war).

Conclusion

The Trump Phenomenon and the Anti-Enlightenment

The Hegel/Marx philosophy paradigm has four components: mediation; totality; genesis; praxis. Utilizing this four part paradigm allows us to conceptualize human history operating as a progressive dialectic – with an end point being a modern, classless society (free of ethnic, gender biases). This is consonant with the Enlightenment view of humanity and the Absolute – whereby the Enlightenment (fairness, justice) is not a function of politics (per se) but of metaphysics.

The content of politics is the Enlightenment versus the anti-Enlightenment. Put differently, the forces of justice, fairness, reason on one side (the Enlightenment) and the forces of domination, oppression, unreason on the other (the anti-Enlightenment). Whereas Marx believed that the triumph of social, political progress was inevitable, the 20th century imparted a different lesson. Namely, that the anti-Enlightenment can defeat, rollback progressive change – for instance, Nazi Germany in the 1930s (Chapter One). During the 1950s in the U.S. the hate of communism (anticommunism) politically overwhelmed the foreign policy moderation of Presidents Eisenhower and Kennedy. One result was the massively destructive American war in Vietnam (Chapter Four). Today, former President Trump and much of the Republican Party invoke hate (xenophobia, white supremacy) and unreason (the putative theft of the 2020 election)[1] to mobilize the public against *socialism, social justice*. A Republican "victory" in 2024 may mean the end of *democracy* in the U.S.[2]

A key aspect of praxis in modern society is popular culture (movies, televison). By definition popular culture has to appeal to the masses, and this means it is not subject to instrumental purposes. Whether or not popular culture "catches on" with the public depends on whether such art is *authentic*. Authentic popular culture requires the freedom of expression. One understanding of authentic art (perhaps especially of popular culture) is that it reflects the values of the Absolute – i.e., praxis.

In popular culture we can identify works that are consonant with the Enlightenment as well as with the anti-Enlightenment. The Star Wars franchise lucidly conveys the anti-Enlightenment, insofar as unreason (the Force) plays a central, dominant role in politics, and social, political change (progress) is absent. The Star Trek franchise (the broadcast iterations) represents a Hegelian/Marxist (Enlightenment) text – whereby it depicts humanity evolving into a highly rational, emotionally mature species (Chapter Two). A fascinating aspect of the Star Trek franchise is that in the late 1960s it was a salient feature of the civil rights and feminist movements (Chapter Three), and later beginning in the 1980s the franchise engages, depicts, critiques the rearguard reaction of the Reagan Revolution.[3] At the core of this ongoing reactionary revolution is the Huntington conception of the *Clash of Civilizations* (Chapter Five).

With popular culture as *Man in the High Castle* and the *Star Trek: Enterprise* episode "Stormfront" (2004) we can see the

---

1   Jeremy W. Peters, "Trump Rally Highlights G.O.P. Split on How to Win in 2022," *New York Times*, Jan. 17, 2022, A16.
2   Jamelle Bouie, "The Trump Conspiracy Is Hiding in Plain Sight," *New York Times*, Dec. 5, 2021, SR7; Jimmy Carter, "America's Democracy Is in Danger," *New York Times*, Jan. 9, 2022, SR4.
3   Jeffrey L. Chidester, and Paul Kengor, eds., *Reagan's Legacy in a World Transformed* (Cambridge, MA: Harvard University Press, 2015).

demoralization that has accompanied the anti-Enlightenment Reagan Revolution – accelerated by post-9/11 politics, which emphasizes *security* to the exclusion of seemingly all other values. This politics resulted in the illegal, wantonly destructive conquest of Iraq, as well as official policies of torture and indefinite detention without trial (Chapter Six). The despair resulting from the absence of an official politics of justice, fairness is arguably the foundation of the Trump phenomenon – an open politics of hate,[4] as well as antipathy toward democracy.[5]

4   Stacy G. Ulbig, *Angry Politics: Partisan Hatred and Political Polarization Among College Students* (Lawrence: University of Kansas Press, 2020); Paul Krugman, "Republicans Say, 'Let Them Eat Hate'," *New York Times*, April 19, 2022, A17, and "Why Did the G.O.P. Become So Extreme?," *New York Times*, June 28, 2022, A23.
5   Reid J. Epstein, and Nick Corasaniti, "They Claim Voter Fraud, Unless It's a G.O.P. Primary," *New York Times*, June 1, 2022, A15; Alexandra Berzon, "2020 Deniers Gain in Races To Run Voting," *New York Times*, June 6, 2022, A1; Azi Paybarah, "Texas G.O.P. Adopts Stolen Election Claims," *New York Times*, June 20, 2022, A13; Stuart A. Thompson, "Right-Wing Radio Sows Doubt About a Vote Yet to Take Place," *New York Times*, July 5, 2022, A1; Nick Corasaniti, "Justice Dept. Sues Arizona Over Voting Law," *New York Times*, July 6, 2022, A15.

Bibliography

Albeck-Ripka, Livia. "A 'Black Box' for an Earth At Risk of a Climate Crash." *New York Times*, Dec. 11, 2021, A8.

Anderson, Terry H. *Bush's Wars*. New York: Oxford University Press, 2011.

Arrighi, Giovanni, with Beverly Silver. *Chaos and Governance in the Modern World System*. Minneapolis: University of Minnesota Press, 1999.

Asselin, Pierre. *Vietnam's American War: A History*. New York: Cambridge University Press, 2018.

Bacon, Michael. *Richard Rorty: Pragmatism and Political Liberalism*. Lanham, MD: Lexington Books, 2007.

Baker, Peter. "Portrait of a Power Grab by a Would-Be Autocrat." *New York Times*, June 10, 2022, A1.

Baker, Peter. "Increasingly Unhinged as Power Slipped Away." *New York Times*, June 29, 2022, A1.

Baker, Peter. "Trump Intent Out in Open." *New York Times*, July 4, 2022, A1.

Barrow, Clyde W. *Critical Theories of the State*. Madison: University of Wisconsin Press, 1993.

Beiner, Ronald. *Dangerous Minds: Nietzsche, Heidegger, and the Return of the Far Right*. Philadelphia: University of Pennsylvania Press, 2018.

Belew, Kathleen. "Militant Whiteness in the Age of Trump." In *The Presidency of Donald J. Trump: A First Historical Assessment*, ed. Julian E. Zelizer. Princeton: Princeton University Press, 2022.

Berkowitz, Eric. *Dangerous Ideas: A Brief History of Censorship in the West, from the Ancients to Fake News.* Boston: Beacon Press, 2021.

Bernardi, Daniel Leonard. *Star Trek and History: Race-ing toward a White Future.* New Brunswick, NJ: Rutgers University Press, 1998.

Berzon, Alexandra. "2020 Deniers Gain in Races To Run Voting." *New York Times,* June 6, 2022, A1.

Bindas, Kenneth J. *Modernity and the Great Depression: The Transformation of American Society, 1930–1941.* Lawrence: University Press of Kansas, 2017.

Booker, Keith M. "The Politics of Star Trek." In *The Essential Science Fiction Reader,* ed. J.P. Telotte. Lexington: University Press of Kentucky, 2008.

Bouie, Jamelle. "The Trump Conspiracy Is Hiding in Plain Sight." *New York Times,* Dec. 5, 2021, SR7.

Britton-Purdy, Jedediah."We're Not a Real Democeracy. That's Why Jan. 6 Happened." *New York Times,* Jan. 6, 2022, A23.

Broad, William J. "Smaller Bombs Raise a Specter of Atomic War." *New York Times,* March 22, 2022, A1.

Broad, William J. "Orbital Fleet Warily Eyes Russia's Atomic Arsenal." *New York Times,* April 6, 2022, A9.

Broadwater, Luke. "Jan. 6 Panel Will Tie Trump To Extremists." *New York Times,* July 6, 2022, A10.

Broadwater, Luke. "Jan. 6 Panel Will Turn Over Evidence on Fake Electors to the Justice Dept." *New York Times,* July 14, 2022, A15.

Broadwater, Luke, and Michael S. Schmidt. "Insider's Account of a President's Volatility." *New York Times,* June 29, 2022, A1.

Bronner, Stephen Eric. *Rosa Luxemburg: A Revolutionary for Our Times.* University Park: Pennsylvania State University Press, 1993.

Brooks, David. "Saving the System." *New York Times,* April 29, 2014, A23.

Bury, Helen. *Eisenhower and the Cold War Arms Race: "Open Skies" and the Military-Industrial Complex.* New York: I.B. Tauris, 2014.

Bush, Billy. "Yes, Donald Trump, You Said That." *New York Times,* Dec. 4, 2017, A21.

Carlson, Darren K. "Public Support for Military Draft Low." Gallup, Nov. 18, 2003. Web.

Carrington, André M. *Speculative Blackness: The Future of Race in Science Fiction.* Minneapolis: University of Minnesota Press, 2016.

Carter, Dan T. *The Politics of Rage: George Wallace, the Origins of the New Conservatism, and the Transformation of American Politics,* 2nd ed. Baton Rouge: Louisiana State University, 2000.

Carter, Jimmy. "America's Democracy Is in Danger." *New York Times,* Jan. 9, 2022, SR4.

Carwardine, Richard, and Jay Sexton, eds. *The Global Lincoln.* New York: Oxford University Press, 2011.

Chambers, Samuel A. *The Queer Politics of Television.* New York: I.B.Tauris, 2009.

Chernus, Ira. *Apocalypse Management: Eisenhower and the Discourse of National Security.* Stanford: Stanford University Press, 2008.

Cheshire, James, and Oliver Uberti. *Atlas of the Invisible: Maps and Graphics That Will Change How You See the World.* New York: W. W. Norton, 2021.

Chidester, Jeffrey L., and Paul Kengor, eds. *Reagan's Legacy in a World Transformed.* Cambridge, MA: Harvard University Press, 2015.

Childs, Peter. *Modernism*, 3rd ed. New York: Routledge, 2016.

Claridge, Laura. *Emily Post: Daughter of the Gilded Age, Mistress of American Manners.* New York: Random House, 2009.

Clines, Francis X. "Reagan Denounces Ideology of Soviet as 'Focus of Evil'." *New York Times*, March 9, 1983. Web.

Cohen, Patricia. "Study Finds Global Wealth Is Flowing to the Richest." *New York Times*, Jan. 19, 2015, B6.

Colaresi, Michael P. *Democracy Declassified: The Secrecy Dilemma in National Security.* New York: Oxford University Press, 2014.

Coontz, Stephanie. *Marriage, a History: From Obedience to Intimacy, or How Love Conquered Marriage.* New York: Viking, 2005.

Corasaniti, Nick. "Justice Dept. Sues Arizona Over Voting Law." *New York Times*, July 6, 2022, A15.

Crary, Jonathan. *Scorched Earth: Beyond the Digital Age to a Post-Capitalist World.* New York: Verso, 2022.

Daddis, Gregory A. *Westmoreland's War: Reassessing American Strategy in Vietnam.* New York: Oxford University Press, 2014.

Davey, Monica. "A Picture of Detroit Ruin, Street by Forlorn Street." *New York Times*, February 18, 2014, A1.

Davis, Julie Hirschfeld. "'Deep State'? Until Now, It Was a Foreign Concept." *New York Times*, March 7, 2017, A19.

de Greef, Kimon, and Sewell Chan. "Setback for U.S. Is Feared as Africa Recoils at Trump Remark." *New York Times*, Jan. 16, 2018, A8.

de Seve, Mike. *Operation Ajax: The Story of the CIA Coup that Remade the Middle East.* New York: Verso, 2015.

Deutscher, Issac. *The Prophet Armed: Trotsky 1879–1921*, Vol. 1. New York: Oxford University Press, 1963.

Dewan, Shaila. "Flawed Autopsies Reflect Biases Even in Death." *New York Times*, June 21, 2022, A1.

Dierenfield, Bruce J. *The Civil Rights Movement*, rev. ed. New York: Routledge, 2014.

Domby, Adam H. *The False Cause: Fraud, Fabrication, and White Supremacy in Confederate Memory.* Charlottesville: University of Virginia Press, 2020.

Domhoff, G. William. *The Power Elite and the State.* New York: Aldine de Gruyter, 1990.

Domhoff, G. William. *The Corporate Rich and the Power Elite in the Twentieth Century.* New York: Routledge, 2020.

Douthat, Ross. "Vladimir Putin's Clash of Civilizations." *New York Times*, Feb. 27, 2022, SR9.

Downs, Gregory P. *The Second American Revolution: The Civil War-Era Struggle over Cuba and the Rebirth of the American Republic.* Chapel Hill: University of North Carolina Press, 2019.

Drape, Joe. "Bankruptcy for Ailing Detroit, but Prosperity for Its Teams." *New York Times*, Oct. 14., 2013, A1.

Duménil, Gérard, and Dominique Lévy. *Capital Resurgent: Roots of the Neoliberal Revolution*, trans. Derek Jeffers. Cambridge, MA: Harvard University Press, 2004.

Duncan, Stephen R. *The Rebel Café: Sex, Race, and Politics in Cold War America's Nightclub Underground*. Baltimore: Johns Hopkins University Press, 2018.

Editorial Board. "Justice for Iraq." *New York Times*, April 25, 2003, A30.

Editorial Board."Rewriting the Geneva Conventions." *New York Times*, August 14, 2006, A20.

Editorial Board."About Those Black Sites." *New York Times*, Feb. 18, 2013, A16.

Editorial Board. "Mr. Trump and Mr. Putin, Best Frenemies." *New York Times*, June 29, 2018, A26.

Editorial Board. "Why Does the U.S. Military Celebrate White Supremacy?" *New York Times*, May 24, 2020, SR8.

Editorial Board. "Ms. Greene Is Beyond the Pale." *New York Times*, Feb. 1, 2021, A20.

Editors of History Channel. *History The 1960's*. New York: History Channel, 2019.

Editors of LIFE. *LIFE The 1960s: The Decade When Everything Changed*. New York: LIFE, 2016.

"Effort to Prohibit Waterboarding Fails in House." Associated Press. March 12, 2008. Web.

Elias, Christopher M. *Gossip Men: J. Edgar Hoover, Joe McCarthy, Roy Cohn, and the Politics of Insinuation*. Chicago: University of Chicago Press, 2021.

Epstein, Reid J., and Nick Corasaniti. "They Claim Voter Fraud, Unless It's a G.O.P. Primary." *New York Times*, June 1, 2022, A15.

Estlund, David. *Utopophobia: On the Limits (If Any) of Political Philosophy*. Princeton: Princeton University Press, 2019.

Fandos, Nicholas, and Sharon LaFraniere. "Two Reports on Meddling: Choose Your Own Verdict." *New York Times*, April 28, 2018, A14.

Fern, Yvonne. *Gene Roddenberry: The Last Conversation*. Los Angeles: University of California Press, 1994.

Feuer, Alan. "A Few Main Characters Form the Core of the Committee's Narrative." *New York Times*, June 10, 2022, A16.

Feuer, Alan. "Gun-Toting Candidate's Ad Suggests Hunt for 'RINOs'." *New York Times*, June 21, 2022, A17.

Feuer, Alan. "Proud Boys Ignored Orders Given at Pre-Jan. 6 Meeting." *New York Times*, June 27, 2022, A24.

Feuer, Alan. "Testimony of Trump Allies And Extremists at Hearing." *New York Times*, June 30, 2022, A17.

Finder, Henry, ed. *The 60s: The Story of a Decade*. New York: New Yorker, 2016.

Fisher, Max. "Thoughts Turn to the Unthinkable: A Spiral Into a Nuclear War." *New York Times*, March 17, 2022, A12.

Flegenheimer, Matt, and Scott Shane. "Bipartisan Voices Back U.S. Agencies on Russia Hacking." *New York Times*, Jan. 6, 2017, A1.

Frank, Robert. "Another Widening Gap: The Haves vs. the Have-Mores." *New York Times*, Nov. 16, 2014, BU4.

Friedman, Lisa, and Jonathan Weisman. "G.O.P. Strategy for Climate Action Is to Delay It." *New York Times*, July 21, 2022, A1.

Gaddis, John Lewis. *Strategies of Containment: A Critical Appraisal of Postwar American National Security Policy*. New York: Oxford University Press, 1982.

Gallagher, Mary Elizabeth. *Contagious Capitalism: Globalization and the Politics of Labor in China*. Princeton: Princeton University Press, 2005.

Gerstle, Gary. *The Rise and Fall of the Neoliberal Order: America and the World in the Free Market Era*. New York: Oxford University Press, 2022.

Gilman, Nils. *Mandarins of the Future: Modernization Theory in Cold War America*. Baltimore: Johns Hopkins University Press, 2007.

Gleijeses, Piero. *Shattered Hope: The Guatemalan Revolution and the United States, 1944–1954*. Princeton: Princeton University Press, 1992.

Goldberg, Michelle. "Trump Shows The World He's Putin's Lackey." *New York Times*, July 17, 2018, A21.

Goldman, Adam, and Shaila Dewan. "Shouting, Smashed Glass, A Lunge, Then a Gunshot." *New York Times*, Jan. 24, 2021, A1.

Gonzalez, George A. *Urban Sprawl, Global Warming, and the Empire of Capital*. Albany: State University of New York Press, 2009.

Gonzalez, George A. *Energy and the Politics of the North Atlantic*. Albany: State University Press of New York, 2013.

Gonzalez, George A. "Is Obama's 2014 Greenhouse Gas Reduction Plan Symbolic?: The Creation of the U.S. EPA and a Reliance on the States." *Capitalism Nature Socialism* 26, no. 2 (2015): 92–104.

Gonzalez, George A. *The Politics of Star Trek: Justice, War and the Future*. New York: Palgrave Macmillan, 2015.

Gonzalez, George A. *The Absolute and Star Trek*. New York: Palgrave Macmillan, 2017.

Gonzalez, George A. *Energy, the Modern State, and the American World System*. Albany: State University of New York Press, 2018.

Gonzalez, George A. *Star Trek and the Politics of Globalism*. New York: Palgrave Macmillan, 2018.

Gonzalez, George A. *Justice and Popular Culture: Star Trek as Philosophical Text*. Lanham, MD: Lexington Books, 2019.

Gonzalez, George A. *Popular Culture and the Political Values of Neoliberalism*. Lanham, MD: Lexington Books, 2019.

Gonzalez, George A. *Popular Culture as Art and Knowledge*. Lanham, MD: Lexington Books, 2019.

Gonzalez, George A. *Popular Culture, Conspiracy Theory, and the Star Trek Text*. Lanham, MD: Lexington Books, 2020.

Gonzalez, George A. " 'May we Together Become Greater' ": in Defence of Star Trek and Anti-Racism." *Foundation: The International Review of Science Fiction* 50, no. 138 (2021): 14–22.

Gonzalez, George A. *Star Trek and Popular Culture: Television at the Frontier of Social and Political Change in the 1960s.* New York: Peter Lang, 2021.

Goodman, J. David. "Told of Injuries, Uvalde Police Still Hesitated." *New York Times,* June 10, 2022, A1.

Goodman, J. David. "Response to Uvalde Shooting Called 'Abject Failure'." *New York Times,* June 22, 2022, A13.

Goodman, Peter S. *Davos Man: How the Billionaires Devoured the World.* New York: Custom House, 2022.

Greven, David. *Gender and Sexuality in Star Trek: Allegories of Desire in the Television Series and Films.* Jefferson, NC: MacFarland, 2009.

Gross, Daniel A. "'Deutschland über Alles' and 'America First,' in Song." *New Yorker,* February 18, 2017. Web.

Gross, Neil. *Richard Rorty: The Making of an American Philosopher.* Chicago: University of Chicago Press, 2008.

Haberman, Maggie, Alexandra Berzon, and Michael S. Schmidt. "Trump's Allies Keep Up Fight To Nullify Vote." *New York Times,* April 19, 2022, A1.

Hafetz, Jonathan. "Don't Execute Those We Tortured." *New York Times,* Sept. 25, 2014, A31.

Hakim, Danny. "Georgia Inquiry Is Subpoenaing 7 Trump Allies." *New York Times,* July 6, 2022, A1.

Hanebrink, Paul. *A Specter Haunting Europe: The Myth of Judeo-Bolshevism.* Cambridge, MA: Belknap Press, 2018.

Harvey, David. *A Brief History of Neoliberalism.* New York: Oxford University Press, 2007.

Harvey, David. *Seventeen Contradictions and the End of Capitalism.* New York: Oxford University Press, 2014.

Harvey, David. *Marx, Capital, and the Madness of Economic Reason.* New York: Oxford University Press, 2017.

Hatzivassiliou, Evanthis. "Images of the International System and the Cold War in *Star Trek,* 1966–1991." *Journal of Cold War Studies* 23, no. 1 (2021): 55–88.

Heale, M. J. *McCarthy's Americans: Red Scare Politics in State and Nation, 1935–1965.* Athens: University of Georgia Press, 1998.

Hinton, Alexander Laban. *It Can Happen Here: White Power and the Rising Threat of Genocide in the US.* New York: New York University Press, 2021.

Horkheimer, Max. *Critique of Instrumental Reason,* trans. Matthew O'Connell. New York: Verso, 2013 [1974].

Hunt, Jonathan R., and Simon Miles, eds. *The Reagan Moment: America and the World in the 1980s.* Ithaca: Cornell University Press, 2021.

Huntington, John S. *Far-Right Vanguard: The Radical Roots of Modern Conservatism.* Philadelphia: University of Pennsylvania Press, 2021.

Huntington, Samuel P. *The Clash of Civilizations and the Remaking of World Order.* New York: Simon & Schuster, 1996.

Hurdle, Jon. "Philadelphia Forges Plan To Rebuild From Decay." *New York Times,* January 1, 2014, B1.

Hurtado, Albert L. *Intimate Frontiers: Sex, Gender, and Culture in Old California.* Albuquerque: University of New Mexico Press, 1999.

INSCOM/ISF (U.S. military intelligence). "Memo: Summary of Information." Nov. 1, 1963, Record # 194-10013-10448.

Irwin, Neil. "Economic Expansion for Everyone? Not Anymore." *New York Times,* Sept. 27, 2014, B1.

Ismael, Jacqueline S. *Kuwait: Dependency and Class in a Rentier State.* Gainesville: University of Florida Press, 1993.

Israel, Jonathan I. *Radical Enlightenment: Philosophy and the Making of Modernity, 1650–1750.* New York: Oxford University Press, 2001.

Israel, Jonathan I. *Enlightenment Contested: Philosophy, Modernity, and the Emancipation of Man, 1670–1752.* New York: Oxford University Press, 2006.

Israel, Jonathan I. *The Expanding Blaze: How the American Revolution Ignited the World, 1775–1848.* Princeton: Princeton University Press, 2017.

Johnson, Paul. *Socrates: A Man for Our Times.* New York: Penguin, 2012.

Jones, Benjamin F., and Benjamin A. Olken. "Do Assassins Really Change History?" *New York Times,* April 12, 2015, SR12.

Kaminsky, Jack. *Hegel on Art: An Interpretation of Hegel's Aesthetics.* Albany: State University of New York Press, 1970.

Kennan ("X"), George F. "The Sources of Soviet Conduct." In *Essential Readings in World Politics,* eds. Karen A. Mingst, and Jack L. Snyder, 3rd ed. New York: W.W. Norton, 2008.

Kennedy, U.S. President John F. "Commencement Speech: American University, June 10, 1963." In *"Let the Word Go Forth": The Speeches, Statements, and Writings of John F. Kennedy,* ed. Theodore C. Sorensen. New York: Delacorte Press, 1988.

Kerbo, Harold. *World Poverty: The Roots of Global Inequality and the Modern World System.* New York: McGraw-Hill, 2005.

Kershner, Isabel. "Eichmann Talks and Talks In Nazi Tapes Riveting Israel." *New York Times,* July 5, 2022, A6.

Kinzer, Stephen. *The Brothers: John Foster Dulles, Allen Dulles, and Their Secret World War.* New York: Henry Holt, 2013.

Klein, Ezra. "The Enemies of Liberalism Are Showing Us What It Truly Means." *New York Times,* April 4, 2022, A19.

Koistinen, David. *Confronting Decline: The Political Economy of Deindustrialization in Twentieth-Century New England.* Gainesville: University Press of Florida, 2013.

Kotsko, Adam. *Neoliberalism's Demons: On the Political Theology of Late Capital.* Stanford: Stanford University Press, 2018.

Kreines, James. *Reason in the World: Hegel's Metaphysics and its Philosophical Appeal.* New York: Oxford University Press, 2015.

Kristof, Nicholas. "An Idiot's Guide to Inequality." *New York Times,* July 24, 2014, A27.

Kristof, Nicholas. "Trump Calls On Extremists To 'Stand By'." *New York Times,* Oct. 1, 2020, A27.

Krugman, Paul. "Nonsense And Sensibility." *New York Times,* August 11, 2006, A15.

Krugman, Paul. "Oligarchy, American Style." *New York Times*, Nov. 4, 2011, A31.

Krugman, Paul. "The Undeserving Rich." *New York Times*, Jan. 20, 2014, A17.

Krugman, Paul. "Republicans Say, 'Let Them Eat Hate'." *New York Times*, April 19, 2022, A17.

Krugman, Paul. "Why Did the G.O.P. Become So Extreme?" *New York Times*, June 28, 2022, A23.

Krugman, Paul. "Crazies, Cowards and the Trump Coup." *New York Times*, July 1, 2022, A22.

Kumar, Anita. "Decoding Trump's speech before the United Nations." *Politico*, Sept. 24, 2019. Web.

Kutulas, Judy. *After Aquarius Dawned: How the Revolutions of the Sixties became the Popular Culture of the Seventies.* Chapel Hill: University of North Carolina Press, 2017.

LaForgia, Michael, and Jennifer Valentino-DeVries. "Fabled Police Force Shows Limits of Death Inquiries." *New York Times*, Sept. 26, 2021, A1.

Lagon, Mark P. " 'We Owe It to Them to Interfere:' *Star Trek* and U.S. Statecraft in the 1960s and the 1990s." In *Political Science Fiction*, eds. Donald M. Hassler, and Clyde Wilcox. Columbia: University of South Carolina Press, 1997.

Latham, Michael E. *Modernization as Ideology: American Social Science and "Nation Building" in the Kennedy Era.* Chapel Hill: University of North Carolina Press, 2000.

Ledbetter, James. *Unwarranted Influence: Dwight D. Eisenhower and the Military-Industrial Complex.* New Haven: Yale University Press, 2011.

Lee, Daniel. *The Right of Sovereignty: Jean Bodin on the Sovereign State and the Law of Nations.* New York: Oxford University Press, 2021.

Leonhardt, David. "All for the 1%, 1% for All." *New York Times*, May 4, 2014, MM23.

Leonhardt, David. "When C.E.O.s Cared About America." *New York Times*, Dec. 3, 2018, A27.

Lerner, Gerda. *The Creation of Patriarchy.* New York: Oxford University Press, 1986.

Levine, Elana. *Wallowing in Sex: The New Sexual Culture of 1970s American Television.* Durham: Duke University Press, 2007.

Lindsay, Michael. *Is Peaceful Co-Existence Possible?* East Lansing: Michigan State University, 1960.

Liptak, Adam, and Nick Corasaniti. "Supreme Court Could Reshape Election Rules." *New York Times*, July 1, 2022, A1.

Lisagor, Nancy, and Frank Lipsius. *A Law Unto Itself: The Untold Story of the Law Firm Sullivan & Cromwell.* New York: William Morrow, 1988.

López, Daniel Andrés. *Lukács: Praxis and the Absolute.* Chicago: Haymarket Books, 2020.

Lukács, Georg. *History and Class Consciousness*, trans. Rodney Livingstone. Cambridge, MA: MIT Press, 1971 [1922].

Marx, Karl. *On the Jewish Question*, 1844. http://www.marxists.org/archive/marx/works/1844/jewish-question/.

Mazzetti, Mark. "'03 U.S. Memo Approved Harsh Interrogations." *New York Times*, April 2, 2008. Web.

Mazzetti, Mark. "Panel Faults C.I.A. Over Brutality Toward Terrorism Suspects." *New York Times*, Dec. 10, 2014, A1.

McCartney, James, and Molly Sinclair McCartney. *America's War Machine: Vested Interests, Endless Conflicts*. New York: Thomas Dunne Books, 2015.

McCourt, David M. *American Power and International Theory at the Council on Foreign Relations, 1953–54*. Ann Arbor: University of Michigan Press, 2020.

McGowan, Todd. *Universality and Identity Politics*. New York: Columbia University Press, 2020.

Mchangama, Jacob. *Free Speech: A History from Socrates to Social Media*. New York: Basic Books, 2022.

McKee, Guin A. *The Problem of Jobs: Liberalism, Race, and Deindustrialization in Philadelphia*. Chicago: University of Chicago Press, 2009.

McMahon, Robert J. *The Cold War: A Very Short Introduction*, 2nd ed. New York: Oxford University Press, 2021.

McPherson, James M. *Abraham Lincoln and the Second American Revolution*. New York: Oxford University Press, 1992.

Menand, Louis. *The Metaphysical Club*. New York: Farrar, Straus, and Giroux, 2001.

"Military draft? Polls finds Americans Opposed." Associated Press, June 24, 2005. Web.

Miller, Carol Poh, and Robert Wheeler. *Cleveland: A Concise History*. Bloomington: Indiana University Press, 2009.

Moye, David. "Donald Trump Appeared In A Playboy Softcore Porn Video." *Huffington Post*, Sept. 30, 2016. Web.

Mullany, Gerry. "World's 8 Richest Have as Much Wealth as Bottom Half, Oxfam Says." *New York Times*, Jan. 16, 2017. Web.

Nash, Susie. *Northern Renaissance Art*. New York: Oxford University Press, 2009.

Nelson, James Carl. *The Polar Bear Expedition: The Heroes of America's Forgotten Invasion of Russia, 1918-1919*. New York: William Morrow, 2019.

Nichols, Nichelle. *Beyond Uhura – Star Trek and Other Memories*. New York: G. P. Putnam's Sons, 1994.

Nielsen, Kim E. *Money, Marriage, and Madness: The Life of Anna Ott*. Urbana: University of Illinois Press, 2020.

Nietzsche, Friedrich. *Beyond Good & Evil: Prelude to a Philosophy of the Future*. New York: Vintage, 1989 [1886].

Noam, Eli M., and The International Media Concentration Collaboration. *Who Owns the World's Media?: Media Concentration and Ownership around the World*. New York: Oxford University Press, 2016.

Notter, Harley. *Postwar Foreign Policy Preparation, 1939–1945*. Washington, D.C.: U.S. Government Printing Office, 1949.

Oshinsky, David M. *A Conspiracy So Immense: The World of Joe McCarthy*. New York: Oxford University Press, 2005.

Ownby, Ted, ed. *Manners and Southern History*. Jackson: University Press of Mississippi, 2011.

Oxtoby, Willard G., Roy C. Amore, and Amir Hussain. *World Religions: Eastern Traditions,* 4th ed. New York: Oxford University Press, 2014.

Ozersky, Josh. *Archie Bunker's America: TV in an Era of Change, 1968–1978.* Carbondale: Southern Illinois University Press, 2003.

Page, Benjamin I., Jason Seawright, and Matthew J. Lacombe. *Billionaires and Stealth Politics.* Chicago: University of Chicago Press, 2018.

Palmer, Bryan D. *James P. Cannon and the Emergence of Trotskyism in the United States, 1928-38.* Boston: Brill, 2022.

Paoli, Letizia. *Mafia Brotherhoods: Organized Crime, Italian Style.* New York: Oxford University Press, 2008.

Parmar, Inderjeet. "The Issue of State Power: The Council on Foreign Relations as a Case Study." *Journal of American Studies* 29, no. 1 (1995): 73–95.

Parmar, Inderjeet. "'Mobilizing America for an Internationalist Foreign Policy': The Role of the Council on Foreign Relations." *Studies in American Political Development* 13 (fall 1999): 337–73.

Parmar, Inderjeet. "'To Relate Knowledge and Action': The Impact of the Rockefeller Foundation on Foreign Policy Thinking During America's Rise to Globalism 1939–1945." *Minerva* 40, no. 3 (2002): 236–63.

Parmar, Inderjeet. *Think Tanks and Power in Foreign Policy: A Comparative Study of the Role and Influence of the Council on Foreign Relations and the Royal Institute of International Affairs, 1939–1945.* New York: Palgrave Macmillan, 2004.

Paybarah, Azi. "Texas G.O.P. Adopts Stolen Election Claims." *New York Times,* June 20, 2022, A13.

Pearce, Kimber Charles. *Rostow, Kennedy, and the Rhetoric of Foreign Aid.* East Lansing: Michigan State University Press, 2001.

Peters, Jeremy W. "Trump Rally Highlights G.O.P. Split on How to Win in 2022." *New York Times,* Jan. 17, 2022, A16.

Petersen, Neil H., ed. *From Hitler's Doorstep: The Wartime Intelligence Reports of Allen Dulles, 1942–1945.* University Park: Pennsylvania State University Press, 1996.

Piketty, Thomas. *Capital in the Twenty-First Century,* trans. Arthur Goldhammer. Cambridge, MA: Belknap Press, 2014.

Pippin, Robert B. *Philosophy by Other Means: The Arts in Philosophy and Philosophy in the Arts.* Chicago: University of Chicago Press, 2021.

Polk, Sam. "For the Love of Money." *New York Times,* Jan. 19, 2014, SR1.

Prados, John. *The Family Jewels: The CIA, Secrecy, and Presidential Power.* Austin: University of Texas Press, 2013.

Raab, Selwyn. *Five Families: The Rise, Decline, and Resurgence of America's Most Powerful Mafia Empires.* New York: St. Martin's Griffin, 2006.

Reel, Monte. *A Brotherhood of Spies: The U-2 and the CIA's Secret War.* New York: Doubleday, 2018.

Rempel, Morgan. *Nietzsche, Psychohistory, and the Birth of Christianity.* New York: Praeger, 2002.

Risen, Clay. "Oris Buckner, Detective Who Blew Whistle on Police Abuse, Dies at 70." *New York Times*, June 9, 2022, B12.

Rockmore, Tom. *Marx's Dream: From Capitalism to Communism*. Chicago: University of Chicago Press, 2018.

Rogers, Katie. "Books Trump Can Praise Without Reading a Word." *New York Times*, Dec. 1, 2018, A18.

Rosenberg, Carol. "War Crimes Hearing Revisits Abuses Meted by U.S. Troops." *New York Times*, May 2, 2022, A8.

Rosenberg, Carol. "Psychologist Describes Fearing for Prisoner at C.I.A. Black Site." *New York Times*, May 4, 2022, A22.

Rosenberg, Carol, and Julian E. Barnes. "Witness Says Haspel, Before Becoming C.I.A. Chief, Observed Use of Waterboard." *New York Times*, June 4, 2022, A17.

Rorty, Richard. *Philosophy and the Mirror of Nature*. Princeton: Princeton University Press, 1981.

Rowe, C. Kavin. *One True Life: The Stoics and Early Christians as Rival Traditions*. New Haven: Yale University Press, 2016.

Rutenberg, Amy J. *Rough Draft: Cold War Military Manpower Policy and the Origins of Vietnam-Era Draft Resistance*. Ithaca: Cornell University Press, 2019.

Sanger, David E. "Scientists Urge President To Slash Nuclear Arsenal." *New York Times*, Dec. 17, 2021, A16.

Sanger, David E., and Julian E. Barnes. "Putin May Be Tempted to Use Small Nuclear Weapon, C.I.A. Chief Says." *New York Times*, April 15, 2022, A8.

Sanger, David E., and Steven Erlanger. "Fear That War Will Spill Over Borders." *New York Times*, April 28, 2022, A1.

Sanger, David E., Eric Schmitt, Helene Cooper, and Julian E. Barnes. "U.S. Makes Contingency Plans Lest Russia Use Its Most Potent Weapons." *New York Times*, March 24, 2022, A10.

Sarantakes, Nicholas Evan. "Cold War Pop Culture and the Image of U.S. Foreign Policy: The Perspective of the Original *Star Trek* Series." *Journal of Cold War Studies* 7, no. 4 (2005): 74–103.

Scharff, Robert C., and Val Dusek, eds. *Philosophy of Technology: The Technological Condition*, 2nd ed. New York: Wiley-Blackwell, 2014.

Schecter, Darrow. *The Critique of Instrumental Reason from Weber to Habermas*. New York: Bloomsbury Academic, 2012.

Schulzinger, Robert D. *The Wise Men of Foreign Affairs: The History of the Council on Foreign Relations*. New York: Columbia University Press, 1984.

Sebell, Dustin. *The Socratic Turn: Knowledge of Good and Evil in an Age of Science*. Philadelphia: University of Pennsylvania Press, 2016.

Security Resources Panel of Science Advisory Committee (a.k.a. the Gaither Committee). *Deterrence and Survival in the Nuclear Age*. Washington, DC: Executive Office of the President, 1957 Nov. 7.

Sellars, John. *Stoicism*. Los Angeles: University of California Press, 2006.

Shane, Scott. "Waterboarding Used 266 Times on 2 Suspects." *New York Times*, April 20, 2009, A1.

Shane, Scott. "Portrayal of C.I.A. Torture in Bin Laden Film Reopens a Debate." *New York Times*, Dec. 13, 2012, A1.

Shane, Scott. "U.S. Practiced Torture After 9/11, Nonpartisan Review Concludes." *New York Times*, April 16, 2013, A1.

Shear, Michael D. "Trump Amplifies 'White Power' on Twitter." *New York Times*, June 29, 2020, A15.

Shoup, Laurence H. "Shaping the National Interest: The Council on Foreign Relations, the Department of State, and the Origins of the Postwar World, 1939–1943." Ph.D. Thesis, Northwestern University, 1974.

Shoup, Laurence H. *Wall Street's Think Tank: The Council on Foreign Relations and the Empire of Neoliberal Geopolitics, 1976–2014*. New York: Monthly Review Press, 2019.

Shoup, Laurence H., and William Minter. *Imperial Brain Trust: The Council on Foreign Relations and United States Foreign Policy*. New York: Monthly Review Press, 1977.

Simpson, James. *Permanent Revolution: The Reformation and the Illiberal Roots of Liberalism*. Cambridge, MA: Belknap Press, 2019.

Singer, Peter. *Hegel: A Very Short Introduction*. New York: Oxford University Press, 2001.

Singer, Peter. *Marx: A Very Short Introduction*. New York: Oxford University Press, 2001.

Slater, Philip E. *Wealth Addiction*. New York: Dutton, 1980.

Smith, Neil. *American Empire: Roosevelt's Geographer and the Prelude to Globalization*. Berkeley: University of California Press, 2003.

Snee, Brian J. *Lincoln before* Lincoln. Lexington: University of Kentucky Press, 2016.

Sneed, David L. *The Gaither Committee, Eisenhower, and the Cold War*. Columbus: Ohio State University Press, 1999.

Steinhoff, James. *Automation and Autonomy: Labour, Capital and Machines in the Artificial Intelligence Industry*. New York: Palgrave Macmillan, 2021.

Stevenson, Richard W. "White House says Prisoner Policy Set Humane Tone." *New York Times*, June 23, 2004, A1.

Stolberg, Sheryl Gay, Nicholas Fandos, and Thomas Kaplan. "Measured Condemnation But No G.O.P. Plan to Act." *New York Times*, July 17, 2018, A1.

Sugrue, Thomas J. *The Origins of the Urban Crisis: Race and Inequality in Postwar Detroit*. Princeton: Princeton University Press, 2005.

Summers, Harry G. "Body Count Proved to Be a False Prophet." *Los Angeles Times*, Feb. 9, 1991, A5.

Talbot, David. *The Devil's Chessboard: Allen Dulles, the CIA, and the Rise of America' Secret Government*. New York: Harper, 2015.

Thorsteinsson, Runar. *Roman Christianity and Roman Stoicism: A Comparative Study of Ancient Morality*. New York: Oxford University Press, 2013.

Trotsky, Leon. *History of the Russian Revolution*. New York: Pathfinder, 1980 [1933].

Ulbig, Stacy G. *Angry Politics: Partisan Hatred and Political Polarization Among College Students*. Lawrence: University of Kansas Press, 2020.

Unger, Craig. *The Fall of the House of Bush: The Untold Story of How a Band of True Believers Seized the Executive Branch, Started the Iraq War, and Still Imperils America's Future.* New York: Scribner, 2007.

Vaïsse, Justin. *Neoconservatism: The Biography of a Movement.* Cambridge, MA: Harvard University Press, 2010.

Van Natta, Don, Jr., Adam Liptak, and Clifford J. Levy. "The Miller Case: A Notebook, A Cause, a Jail Cell and a Deal." *New York Times*, Oct. 16, 2005, sec. 1, p. 1.

Varon, Elizabeth R. *Disunion!: The Coming of the American Civil War, 1789–1859.* Chapel Hill: University of North Carolina Press, 2010.

Vegso, Roland. *The Naked Communist: Cold War Modernism and the Politics of Popular Culture.* New York: Fordham University Press, 2013.

Verene, Donald Phillip. *Hegel's Absolute: An Introduction to Reading the Phenomenology of Spirit.* Albany: State University New York Press, 2007.

Voss, Kimberly Wilmot. *Women Politicking Politely: Advancing Feminism in the 1960s and 1970s.* Lanham, MD: Lexington Books, 2017.

Wallerstein, Immanuel. *World-Systems Analysis: An Introduction.* Durham: Duke University Press, 2004.

Weisman, Jonathan. "Boebert's Call to Ilhan Over 'Suicide Bomber' Remark Shows Chasm Between Parties." *New York Times*, Nov. 30, 2021, A20.

Weisman, Jonathan, and Catie Edmondson. "Republican Censured By a Divided House For a Violent Video." *New York Times*, Nov. 18, 2021, A14.

Welch, Evelyn. *Art in Renaissance Italy: 1350–1500.* New York: Oxford University Press, 2001.

Whippman, Ruth. "We're All in Sales Now." *New York Times*, Nov. 25, 2018, SR1.

Wigelsworth, Jeffrey R. *Deism in Enlightment England: Theology, Politics, and Newtonian Public Science.* Manchester: Manchester University Press, 2009.

Williams, Timothy. "For Shrinking Cities, Destruction Is a Path to Renewal." *New York Times*, Nov. 12, 2013, A15.

Winters, Jeffrey A. *Oligarchy.* New York: Cambridge University Press, 2011.

Winters, Jeffrey A., and Benjamin I. Page. "Oligarchy in the United States." *Perspectives on Politics 7*, no. 4 (2009): 731–51.

Wolin, Richard. *The Seduction of Unreason: The Intellectual Romance with Fascism from Nietzsche to Postmodernism*, 2nd ed. Princeton: Princeton University Press, 2019.

Woods, Jeff. *Black Struggle, Red Scare: Segregation and Anti-Communism in the South, 1948–1968.* Baton Rouge: Louisiana State University, 2004.

Worland, Rick. "Captain Kirk: Cold Warrior." *Journal of Popular Film & Television* 16, no. 3 (1988): 109–17.

Yalom, Marilyn. *A History of the Wife.* New York: HarperCollins, 2001.

Index

PETER LANG
PROMPT

Peter Lang Prompts offer our authors the opportunity to publish original research in small volumes that are shorter and more affordable than traditional academic monographs. With a faster production time, this concise model gives scholars the chance to publish time-sensitive research, open a forum for debate, and make an impact more quickly. Like all Peter Lang publications, Prompts are thoroughly peer reviewed and can even be included in series.

For further information, please contact:

editorial@peterlang.com

To order, please contact our Customer Service Department:

peterlang@presswarehouse.com (within the U.S.)
orders@peterlang.com (outside the U.S.)

Visit our website: www.peterlang.com

Prompts include:

Claudia Aburto Guzmán, *Poesía reciente de voces en diálogo con la ascendencia hispano-hablante en los Estados Unidos: Antología breve.* ISBN 978-1-4331-5207-8. 2020

William Robert Adamson, *Mine Own Familiar Friend: The Relationship between Gerard Hopkins and Robert Bridges.* ISBN 978-1-80079-485-6. 2021

Tywan Ajani, *Barriers to Rebuilding the African American Community: Understanding the Issues Facing Today's African Americans from a Social Work Perspective.* ISBN 978-1-4331-7681-4. 2020

Macarena Areco, *Bolaño Constelaciones: Literatura, sujetos, territorios.* ISBN 978-1-4331-7575-6. 2020

Robin Burgess (ed.), *FRANCESCO ALGAROTTI: AN ESSAY ON THE OPERA (Saggio sopra l'opera in musica) The editions of 1755 and 1763.* ISBN 978-1-80079-505-1. 2022

Desrine Bogle. *The Transatlantic Culture Trade: Caribbean Creole Proverbs from Africa, Europe, and the Caribbean.* ISBN 978-1-4331-5723-3. 2020

Jean-François Caron. *Irresponsible Citizenship: The Cultural Roots of the Crisis of Authority in Times of Pandemic.* ISBN 978-1-4331-8908-1. 2021

Jean-François Caron, *The Great Lockdown: Western Societies and the Fear of Death.* ISBN 978-1-4331-9535-8. 2022

Marcílio de Freitas and Marilene Corrêa da Silva Freitas, *The Future of Amazonia in Brazil: A Worldwide Tragedy.* ISBN 978-1-4331-7793-4. 2020

Mihai Dragnea. *Christian Identity Formation Across the Elbe in the Tenth and Eleventh Centuries.* Christianity and Conversion in Scandinavia and the Baltic Region, c. 800–1600, vol. 1. ISBN 978-1-4331-8431-4. 2021

Janet Farrell Leontiou, *The Doctor Still Knows Best: How Medical Culture Is Still Marked by Paternalism.* Health Communication, vol. 15. ISBN 978-1-4331-7322-6. 2020

Clare Gorman (ed.), *Miss-representation: Women, Literature, Sex and Culture.* ISBN 978-1-78874-586-4. 2020

Eva Marín Hlynsdóttir. *Gender in Organizations: The Icelandic Female Council Manager.* ISBN 978-1-4331-7729-3. 2020

Micol Kates, *Towards a Vegan-Based Ethic: Dismantling Neo-Colonial Hierarchy Through an Ethic of Lovingkindness.* ISBN 978-1-4331-7797-2. 2020

Sunho Kim, *Inner Mongolia, Outer Mongolia: The History of the Division of the "Descendants of Chinggis Khan" in the 20th Century.* ISBN 978-1-4331-8185-6. 2022

Feridoon Koohi-Kamali (ed.), *Exploring Roots of Inequality in Latin America and Peru.* ISBN 978-1-4331-8989-0. 2021

Guy Merchant, Cathy Burnett, Jeannie Bulman, and Emma Rogers. *Stacking Stories: Exploring the Hinterland of Education.* ISBN 978-1-80079-686-7. 2022

Matt Qvortrup, *Winners and Losers: Which Countries are Successful and Why?.* ISBN 978-1-80079-405-4. 2021

Peter Raina, *Doris Lessing – A Life Behind the Scenes: The Files of the British Intelligence Service MI5.* ISBN 978-1-80079-183-1. 2021

Peter Raina (trans.), *Heinrich von Kleist Poems.* ISBN 978-1-80079-043-8. 2020

Josiane Ranguin, *Mediating the Windrush Children: Caryl Phillips and Horace Ové.* ISBN 978-1-4331-7424-7. 2020

Dylan Scudder, *Coffee and Conflict in Colombia: Part of the Pentalemma Series on Managing Global Dilemmas.* ISBN 978-1-4331-7568-8. 2020

Dylan Scudder, *Conflict Minerals in the Democratic Republic of Congo: Part of the Pentalemma Series on Managing Global Dilemmas.* ISBN 978-1-4331-7561-9. 2020

Dylan Scudder, *Mining Conflict in the Philippines: Part of the Pentalemma Series on Managing Global Dilemmas.* ISBN 978-1-4331-7632-6. 2020

Dylan Scudder, *Multi-Hazard Disaster in Japan: Part of the Pentalemma Series on Managing Global Dilemmas.* ISBN 978-1-4331-7530-5. 2020

Wesley A. Stroud, *Education for Liberation, Education for Dignity: The Story of St. Monica's School of Basic Learning for Women.* ISBN 978-1-4331-7911-2. 2021

Geanneti Tavares Salomon, *Fashion and Irony in «Dom Casmurro».* ISBN 978-1-78997-972-5. 2021

Zia Ul Haque Shamsi, *South Asia Needs Hybrid Peace.* ISBN 978-1-4331-9422-1. 2022

Mohammad Rafiqul Islam Talukdar, *Local Government Budgetary Autonomy: Evidence from Bangladesh*. ISBN 978-1-80079-528-0. 2022

Shai Tubali, *Cosmos and Camus: Science Fiction Film and the Absurd*. ISBN 978-1-78997-664-9. 2020

Angela Williams, *Hip Hop Harem: Women, Rap and Representation in the Middle East*. ISBN 978-1-4331-7295-3. 2020

Ivan Zhavoronkov (trans.), *The Socio-Cultural and Philosophical Origins of Science* by Anatoly Nazirov. ISBN 978-1-4331-7228-1. 2020